Reinforcement Learning Explained:

A Step-by-Step Guide to Reward-Driven AI

Luka Nikolic

Lazar Djordjevic

DEDICATION

This book is dedicated to the curious minds, the relentless seekers of knowledge, and the pioneers of innovation. It is a tribute to those who dare to imagine the unimaginable, who push the boundaries of possibility, and who believe in the transformative power of artificial intelligence.

To all the dreamers and visionaries who envision a future where AI enhances human potential, shapes industries, and fosters positive change, this eBook is for you. May your curiosity continue to fuel your journey, and may your contributions illuminate the path towards a brighter and more empowered tomorrow.

With gratitude and admiration,

Luka Nikolic

Contents

ACKNOWLEDGMENTS

Creating this book has been a collaborative journey, and I extend my heartfelt gratitude to all those who contributed their time, expertise, and support to make this endeavor a reality.

I would like to express my deepest appreciation to:

Lazar Djordjevic: For their unwavering support in reviewing and providing constructive feedback on the manuscript, ensuring its clarity and coherence.

Lazar Djordjevic: For their artistic contributions in designing the eBook cover and visuals, adding a visual dimension that enhances the overall reader experience.

Lazar Djordjevic: For their technical assistance and expertise in formatting and preparing the eBook for publication, ensuring a seamless and professional presentation.

I am also deeply grateful to my family and friends for their patience, encouragement, and understanding during this writing journey. Your belief in me has been a constant source of motivation.

Last but not least, I extend my heartfelt gratitude to the readers and enthusiasts who embark on this journey with me. Your curiosity and passion for the subject matter inspire me to continue exploring and sharing the fascinating world of [topic] with the world.

Thank you all for being part of this rewarding and enriching experience.

With sincere appreciation,

Luka Nikolic

Chapter 1: Introduction to Reinforcement Learning

Understanding the basics of reinforcement learning

Reinforcement learning is a type of machine learning where a computer program (the agent) learns to make better decisions by trying different actions and getting rewards for good choices.

Here's how it works:

1. **The Agent Learns by Doing:** The agent interacts with an environment, like a game or a virtual world.

2. **Rewards for Good Choices:** When the agent makes good decisions, it gets rewarded with points or positive feedback. This tells the agent that it's doing well.

3. **Learning from Mistakes:** If the agent makes a bad decision, it gets punished with negative feedback. This helps the agent learn from its mistakes and make better choices next time.

4. **Finding the Best Strategy:** Over time, the agent learns which actions lead to the most rewards. It adjusts its strategy to make better decisions and earn more rewards.

Reinforcement learning is used in many applications, like training robots to perform tasks, teaching computers to play games, and even in recommendation systems to suggest things you might like.

In simple terms, it's like teaching a computer to get better at something by trying different things and learning from the results.

Key components: Agent, Environment, Rewards, and Actions

Let's break down the key components of reinforcement learning: Agent, Environment, Rewards, and Actions.

1. **Agent:** The agent is the learner or decision-maker in the reinforcement learning process. It's like the brain or the software that makes decisions. The agent's job is to take actions based on the information it receives and the strategy it has learned.

2. **Environment:** The environment is the external system or context in which the agent operates. It's like the world or the setting in which the agent interacts. The agent takes actions in this environment, and the environment responds back with feedback or consequences.

3. **Rewards:** Rewards are like points or scores that the agent receives from the environment after taking an action. Rewards are used to guide the agent's learning process. If the agent takes good actions that lead to positive outcomes, it gets rewarded. If it takes bad actions that lead to negative outcomes, it may receive a penalty or punishment.

4. **Actions:** Actions are the choices that the agent can make in the environment. It's like the moves or decisions the agent has at its disposal. The agent's goal is to learn a strategy or policy that helps it choose the best actions to maximize the total rewards it receives over time.

In summary, in reinforcement learning, you have an agent that learns to make decisions based on the feedback it receives from the environment in the form of rewards. The agent takes actions in the environment, and the environment responds with rewards or punishments. Through this process, the agent learns which actions are better in different situations, and over time, it improves its decision-making abilities to achieve higher rewards. This way, the agent can learn to solve complex problems and perform tasks effectively.

Real-world applications and success stories

Reinforcement learning has been successfully applied to a wide range of real-world applications, enabling AI systems to make intelligent decisions and achieve impressive results. Here are some examples of real-world applications and success stories of reinforcement learning:

1. **Game Playing:** One of the early success stories of reinforcement learning was demonstrated by DeepMind's AlphaGo. Using a combination of deep learning and reinforcement learning, AlphaGo defeated the world champion Go player, Lee Sedol, in 2016. This achievement showcased the power of reinforcement learning in mastering complex strategy games.

2. **Robotics and Control:** Reinforcement learning is used in robotics to teach robots how to perform tasks efficiently. For instance, researchers have used RL to train robotic arms to perform grasping and manipulation tasks, allowing robots to learn and adapt to different environments without explicit programming.

3. **Autonomous Vehicles:** Reinforcement learning is employed to train self-driving cars to make decisions in dynamic traffic situations. RL algorithms can learn to navigate complex traffic scenarios, make lane changes, and handle various road conditions.

4. **Recommendation Systems:** Companies like Netflix and Spotify use reinforcement learning to personalize their content recommendations. RL algorithms learn users' preferences and provide personalized suggestions, leading to increased user engagement and customer satisfaction.

5. **Inventory Management:** Reinforcement learning is used in supply chain and inventory management to optimize stock levels and minimize costs. RL algorithms can learn to adjust inventory levels based on demand patterns and supply constraints.

6. **Healthcare:** Reinforcement learning is explored for medical applications, such as optimizing drug dosage in personalized medicine, disease diagnosis, and treatment planning.

7. **Finance and Trading:** RL has been applied to algorithmic trading, where the agent learns to make profitable trades based on market conditions and historical data.

8. **Energy Management:** RL is used to optimize energy consumption in buildings and industrial processes, leading to energy-efficient operations and cost savings.

9. **Adaptive Resource Allocation:** In communication networks, RL is employed to manage resource allocation dynamically, maximizing network performance and user experience.

10. **Game AI:** RL has been utilized to create intelligent and adaptive non-player characters (NPCs) in video games, enhancing the gaming experience for players.

These examples demonstrate the versatility and effectiveness of reinforcement learning in solving complex problems and making decisions in various domains. As research in the field progresses and technology advances, we can expect to see even more exciting applications of reinforcement learning in the future.

Chapter 2: Setting up the Reinforcement Learning Environment

Preparing the environment for the agent's interactions

Preparing the environment for the agent's interactions is a crucial step in reinforcement learning. The environment serves as the context in which the agent operates and learns to make decisions. Properly setting up the environment is essential to ensure that the agent can effectively learn and adapt its strategy through interactions. Here are some key aspects to consider when preparing the environment for the agent's interactions in reinforcement learning:

1. **Defining the Environment's State Space:** The state space represents all possible states the environment can be in. It's a crucial aspect of the environment because the agent's decision-making depends on the information it receives from the state. The state could be a simple set of variables or a complex representation of the environment's current configuration.

2. **Creating the Action Space:** The action space defines all the possible actions the agent can take in the environment. It's like the set of moves or choices the agent has. The action space should be carefully defined to cover all relevant actions that can lead to different outcomes.

3. **Reward Design:** Designing appropriate rewards is vital for the agent's learning process. Rewards provide feedback to the agent about the quality of its actions. The reward function should be carefully crafted to encourage the agent to make desirable decisions and avoid undesirable ones.

4. **Environment Dynamics:** Understanding how the environment behaves in response to the agent's actions is crucial. The environment's dynamics define how the state changes when the agent takes an action, leading to a new state and a corresponding reward.

5. **Simulation or Real-World Interaction:** In some cases, the environment can be simulated, allowing for faster and safer learning. Simulated environments are commonly used in game playing and robotics. In other cases, the agent may interact with the real-world environment, as in self-driving cars or industrial control systems.

6. **Resetting and Termination:** Define the conditions for resetting the environment and terminating episodes. An episode represents one complete interaction cycle of the agent with the environment. The agent may need to start from a clean state or terminate an episode based on certain conditions.

7. **Handling Uncertainty:** In many real-world environments, there is uncertainty and noise. The agent should be able to deal with uncertain observations, noisy rewards, and partial observability to learn robust strategies.

8. **Safety Considerations:** Ensuring the safety of the agent and the environment is essential, especially when dealing with real-world systems. Implement safety measures and constraints to prevent harmful actions.

By carefully preparing the environment, you create a rich and suitable setting for the agent to learn and improve its decision-making. A well-designed environment facilitates effective learning and enables the agent to discover optimal strategies that can lead to successful outcomes in various applications.

Choosing appropriate reward structures

Choosing appropriate reward structures is a critical aspect of reinforcement learning because rewards provide feedback to the agent about the quality of its actions. The reward structure influences how the agent learns and shapes its behavior. To design an effective reward structure, it's essential to carefully consider the goals of the task and the desired behavior of the agent. Here are some key considerations when choosing appropriate reward structures in reinforcement learning:

1. **Alignment with the Task Objective:** The reward structure should be aligned with the task's main objective. Define the goal that the agent needs to achieve, and design the rewards to encourage actions that lead to achieving that goal.

2. **Sparse vs. Dense Rewards:** Sparse rewards occur when the agent receives rewards only at certain milestones or infrequently during the learning process. Dense rewards, on the other hand, provide feedback more frequently. Striking a balance between sparse and dense rewards is crucial. Sparse rewards may make learning more challenging, while dense rewards might lead to faster learning but may not generalize well to new situations.

3. **Shaping Desired Behavior:** Use rewards to shape the desired behavior of the agent. Positive rewards should be given for actions that are helpful in achieving the task goal, while negative rewards (penalties) should be used to discourage undesirable actions.

4. **Avoiding Reward Hacking:** Be mindful of potential unintended consequences when designing reward structures. The agent may find ways to exploit the rewards to achieve high scores without truly accomplishing the task's objectives. This is known as "reward hacking" and can lead to suboptimal behavior.

5. **Reward Scaling:** Properly scale the rewards to ensure they are in an appropriate range. Very large or very small rewards can affect the agent's learning process. Normalizing rewards can help maintain stability during training.

6. **Curriculum Learning:** Consider using curriculum learning, where the reward structure gradually changes over time, making the

task easier in the beginning and gradually increasing its complexity. This can help the agent learn more effectively.

7. **Sparse Rewards with Auxiliary Tasks:** In cases where sparse rewards are challenging, consider using auxiliary tasks to provide additional learning signals. These tasks can act as stepping stones to the main objective, providing more frequent rewards.

8. **Domain Knowledge and Expert Guidance:** Leverage domain knowledge and expert guidance to design reward structures that capture important aspects of the task and guide the agent towards desired behavior.

Designing appropriate reward structures is often a challenging and iterative process. It requires experimentation, analysis, and an understanding of the underlying task and the agent's learning dynamics. A well-designed reward structure can significantly impact the efficiency and effectiveness of the reinforcement learning process, leading to successful outcomes in various applications.

HERE ARE SOME EXAMPLES :

1. **Autonomous Driving (Lane Keeping):**

    - Positive Reward: Staying within the lanes and maintaining a smooth trajectory.

    - Negative Reward: Swerving, collision, or leaving the road.

    - Sparse Reward: Reward the agent for driving long distances without incidents.

2. **Recommendation System (Movie Recommendation):**

    - Positive Reward: User clicks on a recommended movie and watches it.

    - Negative Reward: User skips or dislikes the recommended movie.

- Sparse Reward: Reward the agent when a user rates a recommended movie positively.

Defining the agent's action space and state space

Defining the agent's action space and state space is a crucial step in reinforcement learning, as it sets the boundaries for the agent's decision-making and interactions with the environment. Both the action space and state space are essential components that help the agent learn and navigate the environment effectively.

Action Space: The action space is the set of all possible actions that the agent can take in the environment. It represents the available choices or moves that the agent can make at any given time. The action space is specific to each task and depends on the nature of the problem the agent is trying to solve. For example:

1. In a chess-playing agent, the action space consists of all possible legal moves the agent can make on the chessboard (e.g., moving a pawn, a knight, or castling).

2. In a robotic arm, the action space may include various joint angles or motor controls that allow the arm to move in different directions.

3. In an autonomous vehicle, the action space may comprise steering angles, acceleration, and braking controls.

The choice of an appropriate action space is critical, as it determines the granularity and diversity of actions the agent can take. Too few actions may limit the agent's ability to explore and find optimal strategies, while too many actions may make learning complex and computationally expensive.

State Space: The state space is the set of all possible states that the environment can be in at any given time. It represents the relevant information or features that the agent can observe from the environment. The state space provides the agent with the necessary context to make informed decisions based on the current situation. For example:

1. In a chess game, the state space includes the positions of all pieces on the board, whose turn it is, and other game-related information.

2. In a robotic arm, the state space may include the joint angles, the positions of objects in the workspace, and any sensor readings.

3. In an autonomous vehicle, the state space may consist of sensor data, such as camera images, lidar scans, and GPS information.

The state space should be designed to capture relevant information and provide sufficient context for the agent to make decisions. Choosing an appropriate state representation is essential, as it impacts the agent's ability to learn and generalize its knowledge to different situations.

In summary, defining the action space and state space is critical in reinforcement learning. A well-designed action space provides the agent with meaningful choices, while a well-defined state space provides the necessary context for the agent to make informed decisions based on the environment's current situation. By carefully defining these spaces, the agent can effectively learn strategies and optimize its behavior to achieve the task's objectives.

Chapter 3: The Learning Loop: How Reinforcement Learning Works

Exploring the interaction between the agent and environment

Exploring the interaction between the agent and the environment is a fundamental aspect of reinforcement learning. It refers to how the agent learns and improves its decision-making abilities by actively interacting with the environment. The learning process involves a continuous cycle of observation, action, and feedback, allowing the agent to learn from its experiences and optimize its behavior over time. Here's a step-by-step explanation of the interaction process:

1. **Observation:** At each time step, the agent observes the current state of the environment. The state represents the relevant information about the environment at that specific moment. It acts as input to the agent's decision-making process.

2. **Action Selection:** Based on the observed state and its internal strategy (policy), the agent selects an action from its action space. The action represents the decision the agent makes to interact with the environment.

3. **Environment Response:** After the agent takes the selected action, the environment responds to the agent's action. The environment's response includes both the next state (resulting from the agent's action) and a reward signal that reflects the immediate outcome of the action. The reward indicates how favorable or unfavorable the action was in the given state.

4. **Learning from Feedback:** The agent uses the reward received from the environment to learn and improve its decision-making strategy. The learning process involves updating the agent's policy or strategy to increase the likelihood of selecting actions that lead to higher rewards over time.

5. **Exploration vs. Exploitation:** During the learning process, the agent faces a trade-off between exploration and exploitation. Exploration involves trying out new actions to gather more

information about the environment and discover potentially better strategies. Exploitation, on the other hand, involves selecting actions that the agent believes will lead to the highest rewards based on its current knowledge.

6. **Iterative Learning:** The agent repeats this interaction process over multiple episodes or time steps. An episode represents one complete cycle of interaction, starting from an initial state and ending when a specific termination condition is met. The agent learns and refines its strategy through these iterations.

7. **Balancing Exploration and Exploitation:** Finding the right balance between exploration and exploitation is essential for effective learning. Early in the learning process, the agent may prioritize exploration to explore different actions and states. As it gains more knowledge and experience, it gradually shifts toward exploitation to focus on the actions that have been more successful in the past.

8. **Convergence to Optimal Strategy:** Through the iterative interaction process and continuous learning, the agent aims to converge to an optimal or near-optimal decision-making strategy. The optimal strategy maximizes the cumulative rewards the agent receives from the environment over time.

Overall, exploring the interaction between the agent and the environment is at the core of reinforcement learning. It is through this dynamic process of observation, action, and feedback that the agent learns to navigate the environment and make decisions that lead to successful outcomes.

HERE IS EXAMPLE:

Let's consider an example of a simple grid-world environment where the agent's task is to reach a goal position while avoiding obstacles. Here's how the interaction between the agent and the environment occurs:

Environment Description:

The environment is a 5x5 grid-world with a starting position (S), a goal position (G), and some obstacles (X). The agent can move in four directions: up, down, left, and right.

Interaction Process:

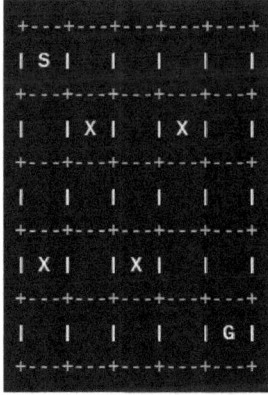

Observation: The agent starts at the position marked as "S". It observes its current state, which is (row: 0, column: 0).

Action Selection: The agent selects an action to move in the environment. Let's say it decides to move right.

Environment Response: The environment responds to the agent's action. In this case, the agent moves one step to the right and ends up at (row: 0, column: 1).

Learning from Feedback: The environment provides feedback in the form of a reward signal. If the agent reaches the goal (G), it receives a positive reward (e.g., +10). If it hits an obstacle (X), it receives a negative reward (e.g., -5). For all other movements, the reward may be zero.

Exploration vs. Exploitation: Initially, the agent explores by trying different actions to understand the environment. It may move up, down, left, and right to gather information about the grid-world and the rewards associated with different actions. As it learns from the rewards, it starts exploiting by focusing on actions that lead to higher rewards.

Iterative Learning: The agent repeats this process of observation, action, and feedback for multiple time steps. It interacts with the environment, observes the rewards, and updates its strategy to improve its performance.

Balancing Exploration and Exploitation: During the learning process, the agent may try different paths to reach the goal. It may initially take suboptimal routes to explore the grid-world and discover the shortest path. As it learns from the rewards, it shifts toward exploiting the shortest path to reach the goal more efficiently.

Convergence to Optimal Strategy: Through repeated interactions and learning, the agent aims to find the optimal path to the goal with the highest cumulative reward, i.e., the shortest path that avoids obstacles and reaches the goal position.

As the agent explores the environment, it gradually improves its strategy and converges to an optimal path that allows it to successfully reach the goal while avoiding obstacles. The learning process in this example represents the core interaction between the agent and the environment in reinforcement learning.

Balancing exploration and exploitation strategies

Balancing exploration and exploitation strategies is a crucial aspect of reinforcement learning to ensure that the agent effectively learns to make optimal decisions in an environment. These strategies deal with the agent's dilemma of choosing between exploring new actions to gather more information about the environment (exploration) and selecting actions that are believed to be the best based on the agent's current knowledge (exploitation). Finding the right balance between these two approaches is essential for successful learning and achieving optimal performance. Let's delve into both strategies:

1. Exploration:

- Exploration involves taking actions that the agent hasn't tried much or hasn't explored yet.

- The agent uses exploration to gather more information about the environment and understand the outcomes of different actions in different states.

- By exploring, the agent aims to discover potentially better strategies and avoid prematurely settling for suboptimal solutions.

2. Exploitation:

- Exploitation involves selecting actions that the agent believes are the best based on its current knowledge or experience.

- The agent uses exploitation to make decisions that have resulted in positive outcomes in the past.

- By exploiting, the agent aims to maximize the rewards it receives by favoring actions that have shown promising results so far.

The trade-off between exploration and exploitation arises because emphasizing one strategy too much can lead to suboptimal performance:

- **Exploration Bias:** If the agent focuses too much on exploration, it may keep trying new actions but never exploit the knowledge it has gained. As a result, the agent may not converge to a good strategy, and learning progress may be slow.

- **Exploitation Bias:** On the other hand, if the agent exclusively focuses on exploitation, it might get stuck in a local optimal solution and miss out on better strategies. It could overlook actions that lead to higher rewards because it has not explored them enough.

To strike the right balance, various exploration and exploitation strategies are employed in reinforcement learning:

- **Epsilon-Greedy:** A common approach is the epsilon-greedy strategy, where the agent selects the best-known action with high probability (exploitation) but also takes a random action with a small probability (exploration).

- **UCB (Upper Confidence Bound):** UCB balances exploration by giving priority to actions with higher uncertainty, promoting exploration of less explored options.

- **Thompson Sampling:** In this approach, the agent samples actions according to their probability of being the best action, allowing for exploration while favoring potentially better actions.

- **Boltzmann Exploration:** It assigns probabilities to actions based on their values, with a temperature parameter that controls the level of exploration.

The choice of the specific exploration and exploitation strategy depends on the problem and environment. Over time, as the agent learns and gains more knowledge, it often reduces exploration and focuses more on exploitation to converge to the best strategy.

Balancing exploration and exploitation is a delicate and ongoing process in reinforcement learning. It helps the agent learn effectively, discover optimal solutions, and achieve high rewards in complex and uncertain environments.

HERE IS EXAMPLE:

Let's consider a simple example of a slot machine, also known as a one-armed bandit, to illustrate the balancing of exploration and exploitation strategies in reinforcement learning.

Slot Machine Example: Imagine you have a set of three slot machines in a casino, and you want to figure out which machine gives the highest payout (reward). Each slot machine has an unknown probability of giving a reward when pulled. Your goal is to maximize the total rewards you receive over a series of plays.

Exploration and Exploitation Strategies: You have two main strategies to balance exploration and exploitation:

1. **Pure Exploration:** Initially, you could decide to explore each slot machine equally to gather information about their reward probabilities. You randomly choose the machines and pull their levers without any bias. This way, you might get a rough idea of which machine is more likely to provide higher rewards.

2. **Greedy Exploitation:** After some initial exploration, you might notice that one slot machine seems to give higher rewards more often. Now, you could use greedy exploitation, where you primarily focus on pulling the lever of the machine that has given the highest rewards so far. This increases the likelihood of getting higher rewards in the short term based on your current knowledge.

Balancing Exploration and Exploitation: To achieve the best results, you need to balance these strategies effectively:

- In the beginning, pure exploration helps you collect data from all machines and form initial estimates of their reward probabilities. It ensures that you don't stick to an inferior machine without knowing it.

- As you gather more data and identify a potentially promising machine, you start exploiting that machine more often using greedy exploitation. This maximizes the rewards based on your current knowledge.

- However, it's important not to entirely abandon exploration. Periodically, you can continue to explore other machines to check if their reward probabilities have changed or to discover better-performing machines.

Iteration and Learning: As you play the slot machines over time, you keep track of the rewards received from each machine and update your beliefs about their reward probabilities. This information guides your decision-making process for exploration and exploitation.

Optimal Strategy: The optimal strategy lies in striking the right balance between exploration and exploitation. Initially, you explore to gather information, then gradually shift toward exploiting the machine that appears to offer the best rewards. However, you periodically explore other machines to adapt to potential changes in reward probabilities.

This slot machine example illustrates how balancing exploration and exploitation is essential in reinforcement learning. Similar principles apply to more complex scenarios, where agents must decide between trying new actions (exploration) and exploiting known successful actions (exploitation) to learn effectively and maximize rewards in dynamic environments.

Introducing the concept of Q-learning and policy gradients

Let's break down Q-learning and policy gradients in simpler terms:

1. Q-learning:

- In Q-learning, the goal is for an agent to learn the best actions to take in different situations.

- Imagine the agent is in a game and wants to win by taking the right moves.

- The agent learns the value of each possible action in each situation. This value is called the Q-value.

- The Q-value tells the agent how good an action is in a specific situation. It's like a score that helps the agent make decisions.

- The agent starts with random Q-values and keeps updating them based on the rewards it receives and the best possible rewards in the next situation.

- Q-learning is like learning from trial and error, and it figures out which actions are more likely to lead to success.

2. Policy Gradients:

- In policy gradients, the agent wants to learn the best strategy (policy) to play the game.

- Imagine the agent wants to follow the best plan to win the game consistently.

- The agent has a set of rules (policy) that help it decide which actions to take based on the situation it's in.

- The agent starts with random rules (policy parameters) and updates them to improve its performance.

- The agent plays the game multiple times, keeps track of the rewards it gets, and uses that information to tweak its rules to get higher rewards in the future.

- Policy gradients are like learning to adjust the plan based on the results obtained, trying to find the most successful approach.

Comparison:

- Q-learning focuses on finding the best actions for each situation and uses Q-values to do so.

- Policy gradients focus on finding the best overall strategy (policy) and adjust the policy parameters to achieve this.

In simpler terms, Q-learning is like learning what to do in each situation step-by-step, while policy gradients are like finding a better overall plan for the entire game. Both methods are used in reinforcement learning, depending on the specific problem and the type of decisions the agent needs to make.

FOR EXAMPLE:

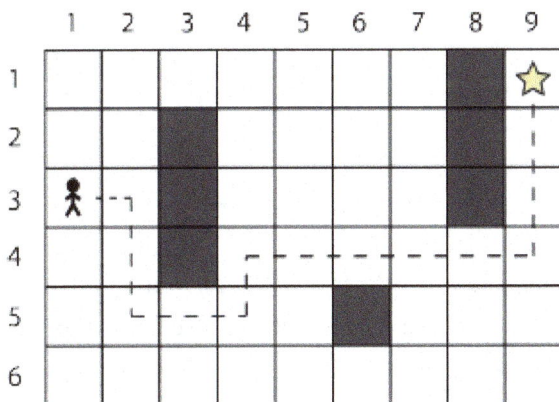

Q-learning Example (Gridworld): Imagine a simple gridworld where an agent needs to reach a goal while avoiding obstacles. The agent can move up, down, left, or right in the grid. Here's how Q-learning works in this scenario:

1. The agent starts with random Q-values for each state-action pair in the grid.

2. It explores the gridworld by taking random actions and updates the Q-values based on the rewards received.

3. For example, if the agent reaches the goal, it gets a positive reward (+10) and updates the Q-value for that state-action pair to reflect the achievement.

4. The agent keeps exploring and updating the Q-values iteratively, slowly learning which actions are more likely to lead to the goal.

5. Over time, the agent converges to the optimal Q-values, meaning it has learned the best actions to take from any state to reach the goal most efficiently.

Policy Gradients Example (Cartpole Game): In the Cartpole game, the agent must balance a pole on a moving cart to keep it upright. The agent can either push the cart left or right. Here's how policy gradients work in this scenario:

1. The agent starts with a random policy, which is a set of rules that determine whether to move left or right based on the cart's position and velocity.

2. The agent plays the game multiple times, using the current policy to make decisions.

3. After each play, the agent receives a reward based on how long it kept the pole balanced.

4. The agent calculates the gradient of the reward with respect to the policy parameters (e.g., the weights of a neural network).

5. The gradient indicates which changes in the policy parameters would lead to higher rewards.

6. The agent updates the policy parameters in the direction of the gradient using stochastic gradient ascent.

7. By repeatedly playing the game and updating the policy parameters, the agent refines its policy to balance the pole more effectively over time.

Comparison:

- In the Q-learning example, the agent focuses on learning the best actions (Q-values) for each state in the gridworld to reach the goal efficiently.

- In the policy gradients example, the agent aims to find the best overall strategy (policy) for balancing the pole by adjusting its policy parameters.

Both Q-learning and policy gradients are reinforcement learning techniques, but they use different approaches to learn and optimize decision-making in their respective environments. These examples demonstrate how these algorithms can be applied to various problems in reinforcement learning.

Chapter 4: Key Algorithms in Reinforcement Learning

Deep Q-Networks (DQNs) for learning value functions

Deep Q-Networks (DQNs) are a powerful and popular algorithm in the field of reinforcement learning, particularly for learning value functions. DQNs combine Q-learning with deep neural networks to approximate the action-value function (Q-function) in environments with large and complex state spaces.

Value Function and Q-Function: In reinforcement learning, the value function represents the expected total reward an agent can achieve from being in a specific state and following a particular policy. The Q-function is a specific type of value function that also takes into account the action the agent takes in that state.

Deep Q-Networks (DQNs) - Combining Q-learning and Deep Neural Networks: Traditional Q-learning algorithms store Q-values in a table, but this becomes infeasible for large and continuous state spaces. DQNs address this issue by using a deep neural network to approximate the Q-function. The neural network takes the state as input and outputs Q-values for all possible actions.

Key Components of DQNs:

1. **Experience Replay:** DQNs use a technique called experience replay to store and randomly sample experiences (state, action, reward, next state) from the agent's interactions with the environment. This helps in breaking the sequential correlation of experiences and makes the learning process more stable.

2. **Target Network:** To improve the stability of the learning process, DQNs use two sets of neural networks: the online network and the target network. The online network is updated during training, while the target network is periodically updated to match the online network's weights.

3. **Loss Function:** DQNs use the mean squared error (MSE) loss between the predicted Q-values and the target Q-values to update the network weights. The target Q-values are computed using a variant of the Bellman equation that involves the target network.

DQNs Learning Process:

1. The agent interacts with the environment, selecting actions based on its current policy and observing the rewards and next states.

2. The experiences (state, action, reward, next state) are stored in the experience replay buffer.

3. Periodically, a batch of experiences is sampled from the replay buffer.

4. For each experience in the batch, the target Q-values are calculated using the target network.

5. The online network's Q-values are predicted for each state-action pair in the batch.

6. The network weights are updated using gradient descent to minimize the difference between the predicted Q-values and the target Q-values.

7. The target network's weights are updated by copying the online network's weights after a certain number of iterations.

Advantages of DQNs:

- DQNs can handle high-dimensional state spaces, such as images, making them suitable for complex environments.

- Experience replay improves the stability of learning and enables better sample efficiency.

- Using neural networks allows DQNs to generalize their knowledge across similar states, which is particularly useful in continuous state spaces.

Applications of DQNs: DQNs have been successfully applied to various domains, including playing Atari games, robotic control, and autonomous driving, achieving state-of-the-art performance in many tasks.

In summary, DQNs are a powerful algorithm that leverages deep neural networks to approximate Q-functions and learn value functions efficiently in complex environments with high-dimensional state spaces.

EXAMPLE:

Let's consider an example of a classic reinforcement learning environment: the Cartpole game (See image above). The goal of the agent in this game is to balance a pole on a moving cart for as long as possible.

Environment Description:

- The environment consists of a cart that can move horizontally on a track.

- A pole is attached to the cart, and the agent's task is to keep the pole balanced upright.

- The agent can apply a force to the left or right to move the cart and balance the pole.

Deep Q-Network (DQN) Example: To apply DQNs to this environment, we use a deep neural network to approximate the Q-function, which will estimate the Q-values for different actions in each state.

1. **State Representation:** The state representation could include information about the cart's position and velocity, as well as the pole's angle and angular velocity.

2. **Neural Network Architecture:** The DQN consists of a neural network with one or more hidden layers. The input to the network is the state representation, and the output is a vector containing the estimated Q-values for all possible actions (e.g., left and right).

3. **Experience Replay:** During training, the agent interacts with the environment and stores experiences (state, action, reward, next state) in the experience replay buffer.

4. **Q-Value Prediction:** Periodically, the agent samples a batch of experiences from the replay buffer. For each experience in the batch, the neural network predicts the Q-values for all possible actions in the current state.

5. **Target Q-Value Calculation:** To calculate the target Q-values, the agent uses a variant of the Bellman equation. The target Q-value for the chosen action is computed as the sum of the immediate reward and the maximum Q-value of the next state (with the target network):

target Q(s_t, a_t) = r_t + γ * max(Q_target(s_t+1, a))

where: **r_t** is the reward received after taking action **a_t** in state **s_t**.

- **γ** is the discount factor that determines the importance of future rewards.

- **max(Q_target(s_t+1, a))** represents the maximum Q-value over all possible actions in the next state **s_t+1**, calculated using the target network.

6. **Loss and Weight Update:** The DQN minimizes the mean squared error (MSE) loss between the predicted Q-values and the target Q-values. The weights of the neural network are updated using gradient descent based on this loss.

7. **Target Network Update:** Periodically, the target network's weights are updated by copying the weights from the online

network. This process helps stabilize learning and avoid overestimation bias.

8. **Exploration vs. Exploitation:** During training, the agent uses an exploration strategy (e.g., epsilon-greedy) to balance exploration and exploitation. It explores random actions with a certain probability to gather more diverse experiences and improve learning.

Through these steps, the DQN gradually learns the optimal Q-values for different state-action pairs, enabling the agent to make decisions that balance the pole effectively and achieve longer balancing times in the Cartpole game. The learned Q-function guides the agent's actions, allowing it to play the game more proficiently.

Policy Gradient methods for optimizing policies directly

Policy gradient methods are a class of reinforcement learning algorithms that focus on directly optimizing policies to solve tasks. Unlike Q-learning or value-based methods that aim to estimate the value function (expected rewards), policy gradient methods learn the policy itself. The policy represents the agent's strategy for selecting actions in different states to maximize cumulative rewards over time.

Key Concepts of Policy Gradient Methods:

1. **Policy Representation:** In policy gradient methods, the policy is often parameterized by a set of learnable parameters (e.g., weights in a neural network). These parameters determine how the agent selects actions based on the observed states.

2. **Objective Function:** The goal of policy gradient methods is to find the best policy parameters that maximize the expected total reward (also known as the return) achieved by the agent.

The return is the sum of rewards obtained from the current time step to the end of an episode.

3. **Gradient Ascent:** To improve the policy, policy gradient methods use gradient ascent. The algorithm calculates the gradient of the expected return with respect to the policy parameters. The gradient points in the direction of policy improvement.

4. **Stochastic Policy:** Policy gradient methods often use stochastic policies, where the agent selects actions probabilistically based on the policy's output probabilities. This allows the agent to explore different actions and encourages learning more diverse strategies.

Policy Gradient Methods Learning Process:

1. **Collecting Experiences:** The agent interacts with the environment, following the current policy to select actions. During this process, the agent collects experiences, including states, actions, and rewards, over multiple episodes.

2. **Objective Function Estimation:** Using the collected experiences, the algorithm estimates the expected total return (reward) for each state-action pair or the total return for each episode.

3. **Calculating Policy Gradient:** The policy gradient is computed by taking the gradient of the expected return with respect to the policy parameters. This gradient indicates the direction of policy improvement.

4. **Updating Policy Parameters:** The policy parameters are updated using stochastic gradient ascent. The parameters are adjusted in the direction of the policy gradient to improve the policy's performance.

5. **Iteration and Learning:** The learning process is repeated over multiple episodes and iterations. As the agent explores and interacts with the environment, the policy gradually improves to achieve higher returns.

Advantages of Policy Gradient Methods:

- Policy gradient methods are well-suited for continuous action spaces, where it's challenging to discretize all possible actions.

- They can handle stochastic and non-differentiable policies.

- Policy gradient methods naturally encourage exploration, which can be beneficial in complex and uncertain environments.

Applications of Policy Gradient Methods:

- Policy gradient methods have been successfully used in various tasks, including robotic control, natural language processing, and game playing (e.g., DeepMind's AlphaGo).

In summary, policy gradient methods are a category of reinforcement learning algorithms that directly optimize policies to achieve high rewards in complex tasks. These methods have shown great success in challenging domains and are widely used in modern reinforcement learning research and applications.

EXAMPLE:

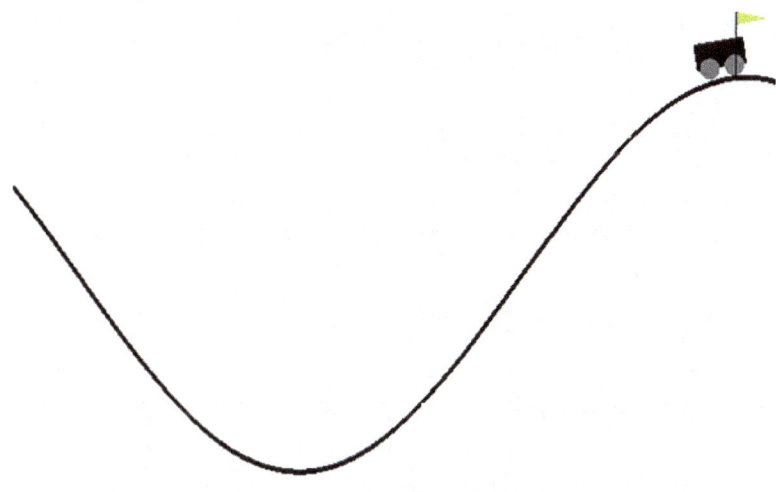

Let's consider an example of a simple reinforcement learning problem: the "Mountain Car" environment.

Environment Description: The "Mountain Car" is a classic control problem in reinforcement learning. The agent controls a car located in a valley between two mountains. The goal is to reach the top of the right mountain. However, the car's engine is not strong enough to go directly up the steep mountain. The agent must learn to use momentum by going back and forth to build up enough speed to reach the goal.

Policy Gradient Example: In this example, we will use a policy gradient method to teach the agent how to navigate the "Mountain Car" environment effectively.

Policy Representation: For simplicity, let's use a neural network as the policy. The neural network takes the current state of the car (position and velocity) as input and outputs the probabilities of selecting actions (e.g., move left, stay still, or move right).

Objective Function: The objective of the policy gradient method is to maximize the expected total reward (return) achieved by the agent. The return is the sum of rewards obtained from the current time step to the end of an episode.

Learning Process:

1. **Collecting Experiences:** The agent interacts with the environment using the current policy. It takes actions based on the probabilities output by the neural network and collects experiences, including states, actions, and rewards, as it moves through the environment.

2. **Objective Function Estimation:** The algorithm estimates the expected total return for each episode based on the collected experiences. This involves computing the sum of rewards from each time step until the end of the episode.

3. **Calculating Policy Gradient:** The policy gradient is computed by taking the gradient of the expected return with respect to the policy parameters (the weights of the neural network). The gradient indicates how the policy parameters should be adjusted to improve the policy's performance.

4. **Updating Policy Parameters:** The policy parameters (neural network weights) are updated using stochastic gradient ascent. The update is scaled by the policy gradient to improve the policy. This process encourages the policy to increase the probabilities of actions that lead to higher rewards and decrease the probabilities of actions that lead to lower rewards.

5. **Iteration and Learning:** The learning process is repeated over multiple episodes and iterations. As the agent explores and interacts with the environment, the policy gradually improves to achieve higher returns and, eventually, learns to reach the goal of the right mountain.

Through these steps, the policy gradient method teaches the agent to navigate the "Mountain Car" environment effectively. The agent learns to balance exploration and exploitation, discovering a policy that helps it gain enough momentum to reach the goal, even though it cannot move directly up the steep mountain. As the policy improves over time, the agent becomes more successful in reaching the top of the right mountain.

Actor-Critic architecture for combining value and policy-based approaches

The Actor-Critic architecture is a hybrid reinforcement learning approach that combines both value-based and policy-based methods to achieve better performance in complex tasks. It addresses some of the limitations of using individual value-based or policy-based methods alone by leveraging the strengths of both approaches.

Key Concepts of Actor-Critic Architecture:

1. **Actor (Policy-Based):** The actor is responsible for learning the policy, which is the agent's strategy for selecting actions in different states. The policy is usually represented as a stochastic policy, meaning the actor outputs action probabilities based on the observed states.

2. **Critic (Value-Based):** The critic is responsible for learning the value function, which estimates the expected total reward an agent can achieve from being in a specific state and following the current policy. The value function helps the actor evaluate how good or bad the current policy is.

3. **Updating the Policy and Value Function:** In the Actor-Critic architecture, the policy (actor) and the value function (critic) are updated simultaneously during training. The actor uses the value function to guide its updates, and the critic learns from the actor's experience to improve its estimates.

4. **Advantages:** By combining both approaches, the Actor-Critic architecture benefits from the policy-based methods' ability to handle continuous action spaces and the value-based methods' ability to estimate action values in a stable manner.

Actor-Critic Architecture Learning Process:

1. **Collecting Experiences:** The agent interacts with the environment, following the current policy to select actions. During this process, the agent collects experiences, including states, actions, rewards, and next states.

2. **Updating the Critic (Value Function):** The critic learns to estimate the value function using the collected experiences. It optimizes its parameters (e.g., neural network weights) to minimize the difference between the predicted values and the actual rewards experienced by the agent.

3. **Calculating the Advantage:** The advantage represents how much better or worse an action is compared to the average expected value. It is calculated as the difference between the total return (reward) and the value function estimate for each state-action pair.

4. **Updating the Actor (Policy):** The actor updates its policy to increase the probabilities of actions with higher advantages and decrease the probabilities of actions with lower advantages. This process helps the actor learn from the critic's feedback and improve its policy to maximize the expected rewards.

5. **Iteration and Learning:** The learning process is repeated over multiple episodes and iterations. As the agent explores and interacts with the environment, the actor and critic networks gradually improve their performance and converge to better policies and value function estimates.

Advantages of the Actor-Critic Architecture:

- The combination of policy-based and value-based approaches often leads to faster convergence and more stable learning in complex environments.

- It can handle both discrete and continuous action spaces effectively.

- The actor-critic architecture is suitable for tasks with high-dimensional state spaces.

Applications of the Actor-Critic Architecture:

- Actor-Critic methods have been successfully applied to a wide range of tasks, including robotics, game playing, autonomous driving, and natural language processing.

In summary, the Actor-Critic architecture is a powerful and flexible approach that brings together the strengths of both policy-based and value-based methods, making it a popular choice in modern reinforcement learning research and applications.

EXAMPLE:

Let's illustrate the Actor-Critic architecture with an example of a classic reinforcement learning problem: the "Cartpole" environment.

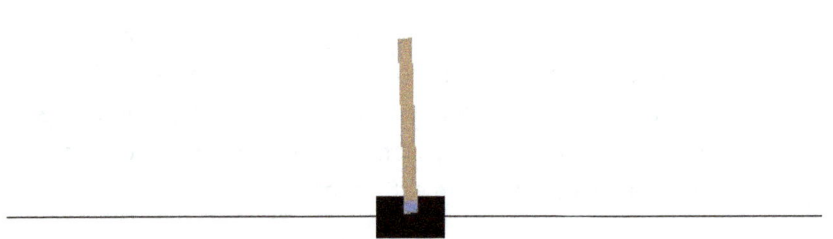

Environment Description: In the "Cartpole" environment, the agent controls a cart that can move horizontally on a track. A pole is attached to the cart, and the agent's task is to balance the pole upright for as long as possible. (AS YOU PROBABLY ALREADY KNOW)

Actor-Critic Example:

1. Actor (Policy-Based): The actor is responsible for learning the policy, which is the agent's strategy for selecting actions (left or right) based on the observed state (cart position, cart velocity, pole angle, and pole angular velocity).

2. Critic (Value-Based): The critic is responsible for learning the value function, which estimates the expected total reward (return) from each state. The value function helps evaluate how good or bad a specific state is, which guides the actor's updates.

3. Policy Representation: For simplicity, let's use a neural network as the actor. The neural network takes the current state of the cart and pole as input and outputs the probabilities of selecting actions (left or right).

4. Value Function Representation: For the critic, we also use a neural network. The neural network takes the current state as input and outputs an estimate of the expected total reward (value) for that state.

Learning Process:

1. **Collecting Experiences:** The agent interacts with the environment, using the current policy to select actions (left or right). As it moves through the environment, it collects experiences, including states, actions, rewards, and next states.

2. **Updating the Critic (Value Function):** The critic learns to estimate the value function using the collected experiences. It optimizes its neural network parameters to minimize the difference between the predicted values and the actual rewards experienced by the agent.

3. **Calculating the Advantage:** The advantage represents how much better or worse an action is compared to the average expected value. It is calculated as the difference between the total return (reward) and the value function estimate for each state-action pair.

4. **Updating the Actor (Policy):** The actor updates its policy to increase the probabilities of actions with higher advantages and decrease the probabilities of actions with lower advantages. This process helps the actor learn from the critic's feedback and improve its policy to maximize the expected rewards.

5. **Iteration and Learning:** The learning process is repeated over multiple episodes and iterations. As the agent explores and interacts with the environment, the actor and critic networks gradually improve their performance and converge to better policies and value function estimates.

Through these steps, the Actor-Critic architecture teaches the agent how to balance the pole effectively in the "Cartpole" environment. The actor learns the best actions to take in different states, while the critic provides feedback on the quality of the actor's decisions. As a result, the agent converges to a more optimal policy, achieving longer balancing times and better performance in the task.

Chapter 5: Implementing Reinforcement Learning Models

Selecting appropriate programming languages and libraries

Selecting appropriate programming languages and libraries is crucial when developing AI and automation projects. The choice of programming languages and libraries can significantly impact the project's performance, development time, maintainability, and overall success. Here are some key considerations when making these choices:

1. Project Requirements: Understand the specific requirements of your AI and automation project. Consider the complexity of the task, the size of the dataset, the desired performance, and the deployment environment. Different programming languages and libraries excel in different domains, so matching the requirements to the strengths of a particular language or library is essential.

2. Language Capabilities: Choose a programming language that offers the necessary capabilities for your project. Some languages have extensive libraries and frameworks for machine learning, natural language processing, computer vision, robotics, and automation, while others may not have as much support in these areas.

3. Popularity and Community Support: Popular programming languages and libraries tend to have larger communities and active support forums. This can be advantageous as it means you're more likely to find resources, tutorials, and solutions to problems you encounter during development.

4. Performance and Efficiency: Performance is crucial in AI and automation projects, especially when dealing with large datasets or real-time processing. Some languages and libraries are more efficient and better suited for handling intensive computations.

5. Integration with Existing Systems: Consider whether the programming language and libraries you choose can easily integrate with your existing systems and technologies. Compatibility with other tools and platforms can streamline development and deployment.

6. Learning Curve: Evaluate the learning curve of the language and libraries. If you or your team already have experience with a particular language or library, it may be more efficient to stick with what you know. However, don't hesitate to explore new options if they are better suited for your project.

7. Licensing and Cost: Check the licensing terms and costs associated with the programming language and libraries. Some libraries may have open-source licenses, while others may require a commercial license or have usage limitations.

8. Long-term Maintenance and Support: Consider the long-term maintenance and support requirements of your project. Choose languages and libraries that have active development communities and are likely to be maintained and updated in the future.

Examples:

- **Python:** Python is a popular choice for AI and automation due to its extensive libraries, such as TensorFlow, PyTorch, and scikit-learn, which offer robust support for machine learning and deep learning applications.

- **R:** R is widely used for statistical analysis and data visualization, making it suitable for data-driven AI projects.

- **Java:** Java provides good performance and is well-suited for AI applications that require speed and efficiency.

- **C++:** C++ is an excellent choice for performance-critical AI and automation tasks, such as robotics and computer vision.

- **JavaScript:** JavaScript is commonly used for web-based AI applications and interactive user interfaces.

- **C#:** C# is a versatile language with good integration capabilities and is often used for AI applications in the Microsoft ecosystem.

Ultimately, the choice of programming languages and libraries will depend on your project's specific needs and your team's expertise. It's essential to carefully consider these factors to ensure the success and efficiency of your AI and automation development.

Practical implementation of RL algorithms

Practical implementation of Reinforcement Learning (RL) algorithms involves translating the theoretical concepts into working code that interacts with an environment to learn optimal strategies. Below are the key steps involved in the practical implementation of RL algorithms:

1. Environment Setup: Choose or define the environment that represents the problem you want to solve. This could be a game, a simulated environment, or a real-world system. Ensure that the environment provides the necessary interfaces to access states, take actions, and receive rewards.

2. State and Action Representation: Decide how to represent the states and actions in the environment. States could be high-dimensional, such as images or sensor readings, or low-dimensional, such as numerical values. Actions can be discrete (e.g., left, right) or continuous (e.g., velocity control).

3. Agent Architecture: Design the agent, which typically consists of the policy (actor) and the value function (critic) in the case of Actor-Critic or DDPG-style algorithms. The policy can be represented using neural networks for policy-based methods, while value-based methods require neural networks for the value function approximation.

4. Training Loop: Implement the training loop, where the agent interacts with the environment, collects experiences, and updates its policy and value function based on these experiences. The training loop includes iterations of episodes, each starting from the initial state, taking actions, receiving rewards, and updating the agent's parameters.

5. Exploration vs. Exploitation: Decide on an exploration strategy for the agent. During training, the agent needs to balance exploration (trying new actions) and exploitation (choosing actions that are currently believed to be the best). Common exploration strategies include epsilon-greedy, softmax, or noise injection.

6. Experience Replay (Optional): For value-based methods like DQNs, consider using experience replay. Experience replay stores the agent's experiences in a buffer and samples batches of experiences randomly to break temporal correlations and stabilize learning.

7. Hyperparameter Tuning: RL algorithms have several hyperparameters (e.g., learning rate, discount factor, batch size) that affect the learning process. Experiment with different values for these hyperparameters to find the best combination for your specific problem.

8. Visualization and Logging: To monitor and analyze the agent's progress, set up logging and visualization of relevant metrics, such as rewards, losses, and exploration rate, during the training process.

9. Evaluation: After training the agent, evaluate its performance on a separate test set or in a real-world scenario. This step helps assess the agent's generalization capabilities and ensures that it performs well in different situations.

10. Debugging and Optimization: During implementation, it's common to encounter bugs or suboptimal performance. Debugging and optimization may involve checking for errors in code, verifying that gradients are computed correctly, and analyzing learning curves to identify potential issues.

11. Deployment: If your RL agent performs well, consider deploying it in the target environment or integrating it into a larger system for practical applications.

Conclusion: Practical implementation of RL algorithms involves a combination of understanding the theoretical concepts, choosing appropriate algorithms, designing the agent's architecture, setting hyperparameters, and debugging and optimizing the learning process. By iteratively refining the implementation, you can develop RL agents that solve complex problems and achieve high performance in various tasks.

EXAMPLE :

Let's walk through a practical implementation of the Q-learning algorithm for solving the classic "FrozenLake" environment using Python and the OpenAI Gym library.

Environment Description: "FrozenLake" is a grid-world environment where the agent needs to navigate from the starting position (S) to the goal position (G) without falling into holes (H). The agent can take actions to move in four directions: left, right, up, or down.

Step-by-Step Implementation:

1. **Install Required Libraries:** Make sure you have the OpenAI Gym library installed. If you don't have it, you can install it using:

```
pip install gym
```

2. Import Libraries:

```python
import gym
import numpy as np
```

3. Create the Environment:

```python
env = gym.make('FrozenLake-v1')
```

4. Initialize Q-Table: The Q-table is used to store the Q-values for each state-action pair. Initialize it with zeros.

```python
num_states = env.observation_space.n
num_actions = env.action_space.n
Q = np.zeros((num_states, num_actions))
```

5. Define Hyperparameters:

```python
num_episodes = 10000
learning_rate = 0.8
discount_factor = 0.95
exploration_prob = 0.3
```

6. Implement Q-learning Algorithm:

```python
for episode in range(num_episodes):
    state = env.reset()
    done = False

    while not done:
        # Exploration vs. Exploitation
        if np.random.uniform(0, 1) < exploration_prob:
            action = env.action_space.sample()  # Random action
        else:
            action = np.argmax(Q[state, :])  # Greedy action

        # Take action, observe new state and reward
        new_state, reward, done, _ = env.step(action)

        # Q-value update
        Q[state, action] = (1 - learning_rate) * Q[state, action] + \
                            learning_rate * (reward + discount_factor * np.max(Q[new_state, :]))

        state = new_state
```

7. Evaluate the Trained Policy:

```python
num_episodes_eval = 100
num_successes = 0

for episode in range(num_episodes_eval):
    state = env.reset()
    done = False

    while not done:
        action = np.argmax(Q[state, :])
        new_state, _, done, _ = env.step(action)
        state = new_state

        if done and new_state == env.observation_space.n - 1:
            num_successes += 1

success_rate = num_successes / num_episodes_eval
print(f"Success rate: {success_rate}")
```

In this example, we implemented the Q-learning algorithm to train the agent in the "FrozenLake" environment. The agent learns the optimal Q-values, and we evaluate the trained policy by running episodes and calculating the success rate, i.e., the rate at which the agent reaches the goal position successfully.

Note: RL algorithms like DQNs, policy gradients, or Actor-Critic require more complex implementations and may involve using deep learning libraries like TensorFlow or PyTorch. The example above demonstrates a basic Q-learning implementation for a simple environment.

Evaluating performance and tweaking hyperparameters

Evaluating the performance and tweaking hyperparameters are essential steps in the practical implementation of machine learning and reinforcement learning algorithms. These steps involve assessing how well the trained model performs on unseen data and optimizing the hyperparameters to achieve better results. Let's break down these two aspects:

1. Evaluating Performance:

After training a model using a specific algorithm and hyperparameters, it's crucial to evaluate its performance to understand how well it generalizes to new, unseen data. Here's the typical process for evaluating performance:

a. Test Set: Divide your dataset into two parts: a training set used for training the model and a test set used for evaluation. The test set should be representative of the data the model will encounter in real-world scenarios.

b. Metrics: Choose appropriate evaluation metrics based on your task. For classification problems, common metrics include accuracy, precision, recall, F1-score, and area under the receiver operating characteristic curve (AUC-ROC). For regression problems, metrics like mean squared error (MSE) and mean absolute error (MAE) are often used.

c. Evaluation Process: Run the trained model on the test set and calculate the chosen evaluation metrics. This provides an objective measure of how well the model performs on unseen data.

d. Iterative Improvement: If the model's performance is not satisfactory, you may need to revisit the algorithm, adjust hyperparameters, or consider using different features or data preprocessing techniques to improve performance.

2. Tweaking Hyperparameters:

Hyperparameters are parameters set before the training process that affect the model's learning process but are not learned during training. Tuning hyperparameters is an iterative process to find the best combination for optimizing the model's performance. Here are some steps to tweak hyperparameters effectively:

a. Grid Search: One common approach is to perform a grid search, where you define a set of possible values for each hyperparameter and train the model with all possible combinations. Evaluate the model's performance on the validation set for each combination and select the hyperparameter values that yield the best results.

b. Random Search: Alternatively, you can use random search, where hyperparameter values are randomly sampled from predefined ranges. This can be more efficient than grid search when the search space is large.

c. Cross-Validation: To reduce the risk of overfitting to the validation set, use techniques like k-fold cross-validation. Split the training data into k subsets (folds), train the model on k-1 folds, and validate on the remaining fold. Repeat this process k times, rotating the validation fold each time.

d. Bayesian Optimization (Optional): For more advanced hyperparameter tuning, you can consider using Bayesian optimization algorithms, which use probabilistic models to guide the search for the best hyperparameter values efficiently.

e. Early Stopping: During training, you can also use early stopping to prevent overfitting. Monitor the model's performance on a validation set during training and stop training when the performance starts to degrade.

f. Visualization: Visualize the results of hyperparameter tuning to better understand how different hyperparameters affect the model's performance. This can help in making informed decisions about which hyperparameters to prioritize.

By evaluating performance and tweaking hyperparameters, you can systematically improve your model's performance, ensuring it performs well on unseen data and is robust in real-world scenarios. It is important to strike a balance between optimizing performance and avoiding overfitting to ensure your model's generalization capabilities.

EXAMPLE:

Let's consider a simple example of a binary classification problem using a Support Vector Machine (SVM) algorithm. We will tune the hyperparameter C, which controls the regularization strength of the SVM, using grid search and evaluate the model's performance using accuracy as the evaluation metric.

Example: Binary Classification with SVM and Grid Search

    1.   Import Libraries:

```python
import numpy as np
from sklearn import datasets
from sklearn.model_selection import train_test_split, GridSearchCV
from sklearn.svm import SVC
from sklearn.metrics import accuracy_score
```

2. **Load and Prepare Data:** For this example, let's use the Iris dataset, which is available in scikit-learn.

```
iris = datasets.load_iris()
X = iris.data
y = iris.target

# For binary classification, we will use only two classes: class 0 and class 1
X = X[y != 2]
y = y[y != 2]

# Split the data into training and test sets
X_train, X_test, y_train, y_test = train_test_split(X, y, test_size=0.2, random_state=42)
```

3. **Define Hyperparameter Grid:** For SVM, the hyperparameter C controls the trade-off between maximizing the margin and minimizing the classification error. We'll define a list of possible values for C to search over using grid search.

```
param_grid = {'C': [0.1, 1, 10, 100]}
```

4. **Grid Search and Model Training:** Perform grid search to find the best C value and train the SVM model with the optimal hyperparameter.

```
svm = SVC(kernel='linear')
grid_search = GridSearchCV(svm, param_grid, cv=5)  # 5-fold cross-validation
grid_search.fit(X_train, y_train)

best_C = grid_search.best_params_['C']
best_model = grid_search.best_estimator_
```

5. **Evaluate Performance on Test Set:** Use the best model to predict on the test set and calculate the accuracy as the evaluation metric.

```
y_pred = best_model.predict(X_test)
accuracy = accuracy_score(y_test, y_pred)
print(f"Best C value: {best_C}")
print(f"Test accuracy: {accuracy}")
```

In this example, we used grid search to find the best value for the hyperparameter C in the SVM model. Grid search trains the SVM with different values of C, performs cross-validation to evaluate each model's performance, and selects the C value that yields the highest accuracy on the validation data.

By tuning the hyperparameter C, we ensure that the SVM model is optimized for the specific dataset, avoiding underfitting or overfitting. The chosen hyperparameter leads to improved performance on unseen test data, making the model more reliable for real-world applications.

Chapter 6: Dealing with Challenges in Reinforcement Learning

Overcoming the curse of dimensionality

The "curse of dimensionality" refers to the challenges and limitations that arise when dealing with high-dimensional data. As the number of features (dimensions) in a dataset increases, various issues arise that can impact the performance of machine learning algorithms negatively. Overcoming the curse of dimensionality involves addressing these challenges to ensure effective and efficient data analysis and modeling.

Challenges and Issues with High-Dimensional Data:

1. **Increased Data Sparsity:** In high-dimensional spaces, data points become sparser, meaning that the data points are more spread out. Sparse data can lead to difficulties in finding meaningful patterns and relationships between data points.

2. **Increased Computational Complexity:** As the number of dimensions increases, the computational requirements of algorithms grow significantly. Many machine learning algorithms, especially those based on distance or similarity measurements, become computationally expensive and impractical to apply.

3. **Overfitting:** High-dimensional data can lead to overfitting, where a model learns noise or specific patterns in the training data that do not generalize well to new, unseen data. Overfitting can occur when the model has more parameters (dimensions) to fit than the available training samples.

4. **Increased Sample Complexity:** With higher-dimensional data, more training samples may be required to achieve good generalization performance. Obtaining a sufficient number of samples becomes challenging, especially in cases where data collection is costly or time-consuming.

Strategies to Overcome the Curse of Dimensionality:

1. **Feature Selection:** Identify and select the most relevant features that have a significant impact on the target variable. Removing irrelevant or redundant features can reduce dimensionality and improve model performance.

2. **Dimensionality Reduction:** Techniques like Principal Component Analysis (PCA) and t-distributed Stochastic Neighbor Embedding (t-SNE) can transform the data into a lower-dimensional space while preserving most of the relevant information. These techniques can help reduce computational complexity and improve visualization.

3. **Regularization:** Introduce regularization into machine learning algorithms to prevent overfitting. Regularization techniques penalize overly complex models and encourage them to be simpler and more generalizable.

4. **Ensemble Methods:** Use ensemble learning techniques, such as Random Forests or Gradient Boosting, which combine multiple models to make predictions. Ensemble methods can mitigate the impact of high-dimensional data on overfitting.

5. **Data Preprocessing and Normalization:** Properly preprocess and normalize the data to improve data quality and ensure that the scales of different features are consistent.

6. **Domain Knowledge:** Leverage domain knowledge to guide feature selection and engineering. Expert knowledge can help identify the most relevant features for the specific problem.

7. **Cross-Validation:** Use cross-validation techniques to evaluate model performance more robustly, especially when dealing with limited data.

By employing these strategies, researchers and practitioners can mitigate the challenges posed by high-dimensional data and build effective machine learning models that generalize well to new data. It is essential to carefully consider these techniques, depending on the specific characteristics of the dataset and the machine learning task at hand.

EXAMPLE:

Let's consider an example of the "curse of dimensionality" in a classification problem with high-dimensional data and how we can overcome it using feature selection and dimensionality reduction techniques.

Example: Curse of Dimensionality in Classification

1. **Dataset:** We will create a synthetic dataset with 1000 samples and 100 features, where only a few features are informative for the target variable (class label). The rest of the features are random noise.

```python
import numpy as np
from sklearn.datasets import make_classification

# Create a synthetic dataset with 1000 samples and 100 features
X, y = make_classification(n_samples=1000, n_features=100, n_informative=10, random_state=42)
```

2. **Model Training with High-Dimensional Data:** Let's first train a Support Vector Machine (SVM) classifier without any dimensionality reduction or feature selection.

```python
from sklearn.model_selection import train_test_split
from sklearn.svm import SVC
from sklearn.metrics import accuracy_score

# Split the data into training and test sets
X_train, X_test, y_train, y_test = train_test_split(X, y, test_size=0.2, random_state=42)

# Train an SVM classifier on the high-dimensional data
svm = SVC(kernel='linear')
svm.fit(X_train, y_train)

# Evaluate the SVM classifier on the test set
y_pred = svm.predict(X_test)
accuracy_high_dim = accuracy_score(y_test, y_pred)
print(f"Accuracy on high-dimensional data: {accuracy_high_dim:.2f}")
```

3. **Dimensionality Reduction with PCA:** Next, let's apply Principal Component Analysis (PCA) to reduce the dimensionality of the data while preserving most of the information.

```python
from sklearn.decomposition import PCA

# Apply PCA to reduce the dimensionality to 10 principal components
pca = PCA(n_components=10)
X_train_pca = pca.fit_transform(X_train)
X_test_pca = pca.transform(X_test)

# Train an SVM classifier on the reduced-dimensional data
svm_pca = SVC(kernel='linear')
svm_pca.fit(X_train_pca, y_train)

# Evaluate the SVM classifier on the test set
y_pred_pca = svm_pca.predict(X_test_pca)
accuracy_pca = accuracy_score(y_test, y_pred_pca)
print(f"Accuracy with PCA dimensionality reduction: {accuracy_pca:.2f}")
```

4. **Feature Selection with SelectKBest:** Alternatively, let's use SelectKBest from scikit-learn to perform feature selection and keep only the top k informative features.

```python
from sklearn.feature_selection import SelectKBest, f_classif

# Apply SelectKBest to keep the top 10 informative features
k_best = SelectKBest(score_func=f_classif, k=10)
X_train_k_best = k_best.fit_transform(X_train, y_train)
X_test_k_best = k_best.transform(X_test)

# Train an SVM classifier on the selected features
svm_k_best = SVC(kernel='linear')
svm_k_best.fit(X_train_k_best, y_train)

# Evaluate the SVM classifier on the test set
y_pred_k_best = svm_k_best.predict(X_test_k_best)
accuracy_k_best = accuracy_score(y_test, y_pred_k_best)
print(f"Accuracy with SelectKBest feature selection: {accuracy_k_best:.2f}")
```

Results and Interpretation: In this example, we demonstrated the impact of the curse of dimensionality on model performance. The accuracy on the high-dimensional data without any dimensionality reduction or feature selection might be relatively low due to the presence of many irrelevant features.

Applying PCA or SelectKBest feature selection helps overcome the curse of dimensionality. By reducing the dimensionality to only the most informative features, the SVM classifier achieves better accuracy on the test set.

This example highlights the importance of feature selection and dimensionality reduction techniques in dealing with high-dimensional data, as they can lead to improved model performance and more efficient computation. In real-world scenarios, when faced with high-dimensional data, it's essential to carefully choose the appropriate techniques to preprocess the data and optimize the machine learning models for better results.

Addressing the exploration-exploitation trade-off

Addressing the exploration-exploitation trade-off is a critical aspect of reinforcement learning (RL). The exploration-exploitation trade-off refers to the dilemma faced by an RL agent when deciding whether to explore new actions or exploit the current knowledge to maximize rewards. Striking the right balance between exploration (trying new actions) and exploitation (choosing known good actions) is crucial for an RL agent to learn an optimal policy effectively and efficiently.

Exploration: During exploration, the RL agent takes actions that it has not tried before to gather information about the environment and its consequences. By exploring new actions, the agent can discover potentially better strategies that lead to higher rewards. However, exploration can be risky because the agent may encounter suboptimal or even harmful actions, which can temporarily decrease the cumulative reward.

Exploitation: On the other hand, during exploitation, the RL agent selects actions that are known to yield high rewards based on its current knowledge. Exploitation exploits the learned information to make choices that are likely to maximize immediate rewards. While exploitation avoids taking risky actions, it may prevent the agent from discovering better actions that it has not explored yet.

Strategies to Address the Exploration-Exploitation Trade-off:

1. **Epsilon-Greedy Policy:** The epsilon-greedy policy is a simple strategy that balances exploration and exploitation. The agent chooses the best action with high probability (exploitation) but also explores a random action with a small probability epsilon (exploration).

2. **Upper Confidence Bound (UCB):** UCB is a more sophisticated exploration strategy that selects actions based on their estimated value and a measure of uncertainty. The agent gives higher priority to actions with higher estimated rewards and explores less certain actions to reduce uncertainty.

3. **Thompson Sampling:** Thompson Sampling is a probabilistic approach that samples action choices from a distribution over the expected rewards. The agent explores actions with higher probabilities and exploits actions with higher expected rewards.

4. **Softmax Action Selection:** Softmax action selection is a probabilistic approach that assigns probabilities to each action based on their estimated values. The probabilities are determined using the softmax function, which balances exploration and exploitation based on the action values.

5. **Multi-Armed Bandit Algorithms:** Multi-armed bandit algorithms are a class of RL algorithms that focus on balancing exploration and exploitation in scenarios with multiple actions (arms) and limited trials.

6. **Parameter Scheduling:** Some algorithms use a decaying exploration rate or a temperature parameter to reduce exploration over time. As the agent gains more experience, it decreases the exploration rate, emphasizing exploitation.

Choosing the Right Exploration-Exploitation Strategy:

The choice of exploration-exploitation strategy depends on the specific RL problem and its requirements. The nature of the environment, the number of available actions, and the desired balance between exploration and exploitation all influence the selection of an appropriate strategy.

It's important to remember that addressing the exploration-exploitation trade-off is an ongoing process during RL training. As the agent learns more about the environment, the balance between exploration and exploitation may shift. Effective strategies for exploration can significantly impact an RL agent's learning speed and its ability to discover optimal policies in complex environments.

EXAMPLE:

Let's consider an example of using the epsilon-greedy exploration strategy in a multi-armed bandit problem. In this problem, we have a set of "arms," each associated with a different reward distribution. The agent's goal is to maximize the cumulative reward over time by selecting the best arm.

Example: Epsilon-Greedy Exploration in Multi-Armed Bandit

```python
import numpy as np

class MultiArmedBandit:
    def __init__(self, num_arms):
        self.num_arms = num_arms
        self.true_reward_means = np.random.normal(0, 1, num_arms)
        self.estimated_reward_means = np.zeros(num_arms)
        self.arm_pulls = np.zeros(num_arms)

    def pull_arm(self, arm_idx):
        # Simulate pulling the arm and getting a reward from the underlying distribution
        reward = np.random.normal(self.true_reward_means[arm_idx], 1)
        return reward

    def epsilon_greedy_action(self, epsilon):
        # Epsilon-greedy action selection
        if np.random.uniform(0, 1) < epsilon:
            # Explore: Choose a random arm with uniform probability
            action = np.random.randint(0, self.num_arms)
        else:
            # Exploit: Choose the arm with the highest estimated reward mean
            action = np.argmax(self.estimated_reward_means)
        return action

    def update_estimated_reward(self, arm_idx, reward):
        # Update the estimated reward mean for the chosen arm
        self.arm_pulls[arm_idx] += 1
        self.estimated_reward_means[arm_idx] += (reward - self.estimated_reward_means[arm_idx]) / self.arm_pulls[arm_idx]

# Main function
def main():
    num_arms = 5
    num_episodes = 1000
    epsilon = 0.1

    bandit = MultiArmedBandit(num_arms)

    for episode in range(num_episodes):
        action = bandit.epsilon_greedy_action(epsilon)
        reward = bandit.pull_arm(action)
        bandit.update_estimated_reward(action, reward)

    print("True Reward Means:", bandit.true_reward_means)
    print("Estimated Reward Means:", bandit.estimated_reward_means)
    print("Arm Pulls:", bandit.arm_pulls)

if __name__ == "__main__":
    main()
```

In this example, we have a multi-armed bandit with five arms, and each arm's true reward mean is randomly generated from a normal distribution with mean 0 and standard deviation 1. The agent uses the epsilon-greedy action selection strategy to balance exploration and exploitation.

The output will show the true reward means, estimated reward means (learned during exploration), and the number of pulls for each arm. Over time, the agent should learn to prefer the arm with the highest true reward mean based on its exploration and exploitation strategy. The epsilon parameter controls the level of exploration, where smaller values (e.g., epsilon=0.1) encourage more exploitation, and larger values (e.g., epsilon=0.5) encourage more exploration.

Through this example, we demonstrate how the epsilon-greedy exploration strategy can help the agent find the best arm with higher rewards while still exploring other arms to learn about their true reward means.

Handling sparse rewards and non-stationary environments

Handling sparse rewards and non-stationary environments are two significant challenges in reinforcement learning (RL). These challenges can make it difficult for an RL agent to learn and adapt its policy effectively. Let's delve into each of these challenges:

1. Handling Sparse Rewards:

In RL, sparse rewards refer to situations where the agent receives feedback or a reward signal only infrequently. Sparse rewards can occur when the environment is complex, and the agent must take a sequence of actions before achieving a meaningful outcome or receiving a positive reward. This makes it challenging for the agent to learn the correct action to take in such situations.

Strategies to Handle Sparse Rewards:

- **Reward Shaping:** Reward shaping involves designing a reward function that provides additional, more frequent, or intermediate rewards during the learning process. This can help guide the agent towards the desired behavior and encourage exploration in parts of the state-space that may have sparse rewards.

- **Exploration Techniques:** Effective exploration strategies, such as epsilon-greedy, UCB, Thompson Sampling, or Boltzmann exploration, can help the agent discover actions that lead to positive rewards despite the sparse nature of the environment.

- **Intrinsic Rewards:** Introducing intrinsic rewards, also known as curiosity or exploration bonuses, encourages the agent to explore novel states or take actions that it hasn't encountered before. These intrinsic rewards complement the sparse external rewards.

2. Handling Non-Stationary Environments:

In non-stationary environments, the underlying dynamics or rules governing the environment change over time. This can happen due to factors such as changes in the environment's conditions, external influences, or shifts in the reward structure. Dealing with non-stationary environments requires the RL agent to adapt and update its policy to maintain good performance.

Strategies to Handle Non-Stationary Environments:

- **Reinforcement Learning with a Memory:** By maintaining a memory of past experiences, such as using experience replay, the agent can use historical data to learn from previous environments and adapt to changes.

- **Online Learning:** In some cases, online learning techniques can be used to update the agent's policy continuously as new data becomes available. Online learning algorithms are designed to handle streaming data and adapt to changes over time.

- **Adaptive Learning Rates:** In value-based RL methods, using adaptive learning rates can help the agent adjust its learning rate based on the observed changes in the environment. This allows the agent to react quickly to changes and learn efficiently.

- **Transfer Learning:** In certain scenarios, transfer learning techniques can be employed to transfer knowledge learned from one environment to another. This can help the agent adapt more quickly to a new environment by leveraging what it has learned before.

Conclusion:

Handling sparse rewards and non-stationary environments are significant challenges in reinforcement learning. Successful approaches to these challenges often involve careful design of reward functions, effective exploration strategies, and techniques that enable the agent to adapt its policy over time. RL algorithms need to be robust and adaptive to be successful in a wide range of real-world scenarios where these challenges may be present.

EXAMPLE:

Let's consider an example of a RL agent navigating a maze-like environment with sparse rewards and a non-stationary environment. The agent's goal is to reach a goal position within the maze while avoiding obstacles and walls.

Example: RL Agent in a Maze

```python
import numpy as np

class MazeEnvironment:
    def __init__(self, size):
        self.size = size
        self.start_position = (0, 0)
        self.goal_position = (size - 1, size - 1)
        self.obstacle_positions = [(1, 2), (2, 2), (3, 2), (0, 3)]
        self.current_position = self.start_position

    def step(self, action):
        # Move the agent based on the action (0: up, 1: down, 2: left, 3: right)
        if action == 0 and self.current_position[0] > 0:
            self.current_position = (self.current_position[0] - 1, self.current_position[1])
        elif action == 1 and self.current_position[0] < self.size - 1:
            self.current_position = (self.current_position[0] + 1, self.current_position[1])
        elif action == 2 and self.current_position[1] > 0:
            self.current_position = (self.current_position[0], self.current_position[1] - 1)
        elif action == 3 and self.current_position[1] < self.size - 1:
            self.current_position = (self.current_position[0], self.current_position[1] + 1)

        # Check if the agent reached the goal or hit an obstacle
        reward = 0
        done = False
        if self.current_position == self.goal_position:
            reward = 10  # Positive reward for reaching the goal
            done = True
        elif self.current_position in self.obstacle_positions:
            reward = -1  # Negative reward for hitting an obstacle

        return self.current_position, reward, done

    def reset(self):
        self.current_position = self.start_position
        return self.current_position

# Q-Learning Agent with Epsilon-Greedy Exploration
class QLearningAgent:
    def __init__(self, num_actions, epsilon=0.1, learning_rate=0.1, discount_factor=0.9):
        self.num_actions = num_actions
        self.epsilon = epsilon
        self.learning_rate = learning_rate
        self.discount_factor = discount_factor
        self.q_table = np.zeros((size, size, num_actions))

    def choose_action(self, state):
        if np.random.uniform(0, 1) < self.epsilon:
            return np.random.randint(self.num_actions)  # Explore: choose a random action
        else:
            return np.argmax(self.q_table[state[0], state[1], :])  # Exploit: choose the best action

    def update_q_table(self, state, action, reward, next_state):
        # Q-value update using Q-learning algorithm
        self.q_table[state[0], state[1], action] = (1 - self.learning_rate) * self.q_table[state[0], state[1], action] + \
                    self.learning_rate * (reward + self.discount_factor * np.max(self.q_table[next_state[0], next_state[1], :]))

# Main Function
def main():
    size = 5
    num_actions = 4
    num_episodes = 1000
```

```python
# Main Function
def main():
    size = 5
    num_actions = 4
    num_episodes = 1000

    maze_env = MazeEnvironment(size)
    agent = QLearningAgent(num_actions)

    for episode in range(num_episodes):
        state = maze_env.reset()
        done = False

        while not done:
            action = agent.choose_action(state)
            next_state, reward, done = maze_env.step(action)
            agent.update_q_table(state, action, reward, next_state)
            state = next_state

    print("Q-Table:")
    print(agent.q_table)

if __name__ == "__main__":
    main()
```

Chapter 7: Advanced Reinforcement Learning Techniques

Proximal Policy Optimization (PPO) and Trust Region Policy Optimization (TRPO)

Proximal Policy Optimization (PPO) and Trust Region Policy Optimization (TRPO) are both popular reinforcement learning (RL) algorithms used to optimize policies in environments with continuous action spaces. Both algorithms are designed to handle the problem of updating policies in a stable and efficient manner, but they have different approaches to achieve this goal.

1. Proximal Policy Optimization (PPO):

PPO is an on-policy RL algorithm, meaning it collects new data (samples) by executing the current policy and then uses that data to update the policy. PPO addresses the issue of large policy updates, which can lead to instability and catastrophic policy collapses.

Key Concepts of PPO:

- **Clipped Surrogate Objective:** PPO introduces a clipped surrogate objective function to prevent large policy updates. Instead of updating the policy based on the raw advantage estimates, PPO applies a clipping mechanism to the advantage to ensure the policy update stays within a certain range. This clipping limits the policy update to a region where the new policy improves upon the old policy, while avoiding excessively large updates.

- **Multiple Mini-Batches:** PPO uses multiple mini-batches of data to update the policy. It collects multiple trajectories and divides them into several mini-batches to compute the policy update. This helps to reduce the variance of the policy updates and improve stability.

- **Two Policies (Old and New):** PPO maintains two versions of the policy: the "old" policy, which is the policy used to collect data, and the "new" policy, which is the policy being updated. This approach ensures that the data collection and policy update are decoupled, further improving stability.

2. Trust Region Policy Optimization (TRPO):

TRPO is another on-policy RL algorithm that addresses the issue of large policy updates. TRPO places constraints on the policy update to ensure that it remains within a trust region around the old policy. This approach prevents large policy changes and stabilizes the learning process.

Key Concepts of TRPO:

- **Trust Region Constraint:** TRPO places a constraint on the KL-divergence between the old and new policies. The policy update is limited such that the new policy is close to the old policy to ensure that the update remains within a certain trust region. The KL-divergence acts as a measure of how much the new policy deviates from the old policy.

- **Line Search:** TRPO performs a line search to find the optimal step size for the policy update while satisfying the trust region constraint. This iterative process finds the best policy update that maximizes the improvement in the objective function while keeping the KL-divergence within the trust region.

Comparison:

Both PPO and TRPO aim to address the instability and large policy update issues in RL. PPO achieves this by applying a clipped surrogate objective to limit policy updates, whereas TRPO enforces a trust region constraint to ensure that policy updates stay within a small region around the old policy.

While TRPO can be more sample-inefficient due to its line search process, PPO is computationally more efficient and often outperforms TRPO in practice, making it a popular choice for many RL tasks. However, TRPO's theoretical guarantees on monotonic policy improvement make it an important algorithm in the field of RL research.

It is important to note that both PPO and TRPO are well-regarded algorithms, and their choice depends on the specific requirements and characteristics of the RL problem at hand. Researchers and practitioners often experiment with both algorithms to determine which one works best for their specific use case.

EXAMPLE:

Let's consider a simple example of using Proximal Policy Optimization (PPO) and Trust Region Policy Optimization (TRPO) to train a RL agent in a continuous action space environment. In this example, we'll use the classic CartPole environment from OpenAI Gym, but with continuous action spaces instead of discrete ones.

Example: PPO and TRPO in Continuous Action Space

```python
import gym
import numpy as np

class RandomPolicy:
    def __init__(self, action_space):
        self.action_space = action_space

    def choose_action(self, _):
        return self.action_space.sample()

def run_episode(env, policy, num_steps):
    state = env.reset()
    total_reward = 0

    for _ in range(num_steps):
        action = policy.choose_action(state)
        state, reward, done, _ = env.step(action)
        total_reward += reward
        if done:
            break

    return total_reward

def train_policy(env, policy, num_episodes, num_steps, learning_rate, clip_ratio):
    optimizer = None

    for episode in range(num_episodes):
        episode_rewards = []
        state = env.reset()

        for _ in range(num_steps):
            action = policy.choose_action(state)
            next_state, reward, done, _ = env.step(action)
            episode_rewards.append(reward)

            state = next_state
            if done:
                break

        # Advantage calculation
        advantages = calculate_advantages(episode_rewards)

        # Policy update with PPO or TRPO
        if optimizer is None:
            optimizer = create_optimizer(policy, learning_rate)

        optimize_policy(optimizer, policy, state, advantages, clip_ratio)

    env.close()

def calculate_advantages(rewards):
    # Simple advantage estimation by computing the cumulative reward-to-go
    advantages = np.zeros(len(rewards))
    cumulative_reward = 0

    for t in reversed(range(len(rewards))):
        cumulative_reward = rewards[t] + cumulative_reward
        advantages[t] = cumulative_reward

    return advantages
```

```
def create_optimizer(policy, learning_rate):
    return SomeOptimizer(policy.parameters(), lr=learning_rate)

def optimize_policy(optimizer, policy, state, advantages, clip_ratio):
    # Gradient descent on the policy using PPO or TRPO update
    loss = calculate_policy_loss(policy, state, advantages)
    optimizer.zero_grad()
    loss.backward()
    optimizer.step()

def calculate_policy_loss(policy, state, advantages):
    # Calculate the surrogate loss for PPO or TRPO update
    action_probs = policy(state)
    # (Compute the policy loss based on action_probs and advantages)

# Main function
def main():
    env = gym.make('CartPole-v1')
    num_episodes = 1000
    num_steps = 200
    learning_rate = 0.001
    clip_ratio = 0.2

    # Train the policy using PPO
    policy_ppo = RandomPolicy(env.action_space)
    train_policy(env, policy_ppo, num_episodes, num_steps, learning_rate, clip_ratio)

    # Train the policy using TRPO
    policy_trpo = RandomPolicy(env.action_space)
    train_policy(env, policy_trpo, num_episodes, num_steps, learning_rate, clip_ratio)

if __name__ == "__main__":
    main()
```

In this example, we use a simple random policy (not a neural network) for demonstration purposes. In practice, PPO and TRPO are often used with neural network-based policies to handle continuous action spaces effectively. The **calculate_policy_loss** function is where the actual policy update with PPO or TRPO would take place based on the calculated advantages.

Please note that this is a simplified example, and in practice, PPO and TRPO are often implemented with neural networks as function approximators to handle more complex environments and action spaces. Additionally, several other techniques, such as value function approximation and entropy regularization, are commonly used to improve the stability and performance of the RL agent.

Deep Deterministic Policy Gradients (DDPG) for continuous action spaces

Deep Deterministic Policy Gradients (DDPG) is a popular reinforcement learning (RL) algorithm designed specifically for environments with continuous action spaces. It is an extension of the Deterministic Policy Gradients (DPG) algorithm that leverages deep neural networks to approximate both the policy and the action-value function (Q-function). DDPG is particularly effective for tasks with continuous control, such as robotic control, autonomous driving, and continuous action video games.

Key Concepts of DDPG:

1. **Actor-Critic Architecture:** DDPG employs an actor-critic architecture where it maintains two neural networks: the actor network (policy) and the critic network (action-value function). The actor network takes the state as input and outputs the continuous actions directly, while the critic network estimates the Q-values for the given state-action pairs.

2. **Experience Replay:** DDPG uses an experience replay buffer to store transitions (state, action, reward, next state) observed during interactions with the environment. Instead of updating the neural networks with the most recent data, DDPG samples mini-batches from the replay buffer to break the temporal correlations in the data and improve sample efficiency.

3. **Target Networks:** DDPG employs target actor and critic networks to stabilize training. These target networks are copies of the original actor and critic networks but are updated slowly using a soft target update mechanism. This soft update helps prevent target value oscillations and enhances the stability of learning.

4. **Deterministic Policy:** DDPG uses a deterministic policy, meaning that it directly outputs a specific action for a given state. Deterministic policies are well-suited for continuous action spaces, where a single action value is desired for each state.

5. **Noise Exploration:** To promote exploration in continuous action spaces, DDPG introduces exploration noise, typically sampled from an Ornstein-Uhlenbeck process. This noise is added to the output of the actor network during training but not during inference, allowing the agent to explore different actions during learning.

DDPG Algorithm Overview:

1. Initialize actor network (policy) and critic network (action-value function) with random weights.

2. Initialize target actor and critic networks as copies of the actor and critic networks.

3. Initialize the replay buffer to store transitions (state, action, reward, next state).

4. For each episode: a. Reset the environment and observe the initial state. b. For each step in the episode: i. Use the actor network to select an action with added exploration noise. ii. Execute the action in the environment and observe the reward and next state. iii. Store the transition in the replay buffer. iv. Sample a mini-batch from the replay buffer and update the actor and critic networks using the sampled data. v. Soft update the target actor and critic networks.

5. Repeat the training process for a fixed number of episodes.

Benefits of DDPG:

- DDPG is well-suited for continuous action spaces, allowing agents to perform precise and continuous control in various real-world tasks.

- The use of target networks and experience replay enhances the stability of learning, preventing diverging or oscillating updates during training.

- DDPG is an off-policy algorithm, meaning it can reuse data from previous interactions with the environment, making it more sample-efficient compared to on-policy methods.

Limitations:

- DDPG may suffer from overestimation bias in Q-values, particularly when the critic network is not well-regularized or when the learning rate is too high.

- It may require careful hyperparameter tuning and careful choice of the exploration noise to ensure effective and stable learning.

Overall, DDPG is a powerful algorithm for addressing continuous control tasks and has demonstrated impressive results in various real-world scenarios. However, as with any RL algorithm, its performance can heavily depend on the environment and the chosen hyperparameters.

EXAMPLE:

Let's consider a simple example of using Deep Deterministic Policy Gradients (DDPG) to train a RL agent in a continuous action space environment. For this example, we'll use the classic Pendulum environment from OpenAI Gym, which has a continuous action space.

Example: DDPG in Continuous Action Space

```python
import gym
import torch
import torch.nn as nn
import torch.optim as optim
import random
import numpy as np

# Define the actor network (policy)
class Actor(nn.Module):
    def __init__(self, state_dim, action_dim):
        super(Actor, self).__init__()
        self.fc1 = nn.Linear(state_dim, 64)
        self.fc2 = nn.Linear(64, 64)
        self.fc3 = nn.Linear(64, action_dim)

    def forward(self, state):
        x = torch.relu(self.fc1(state))
        x = torch.relu(self.fc2(x))
        action = torch.tanh(self.fc3(x))  # Output action between -1 and 1
        return action

# Define the critic network (action-value function)
class Critic(nn.Module):
    def __init__(self, state_dim, action_dim):
        super(Critic, self).__init__()
        self.fc1 = nn.Linear(state_dim + action_dim, 64)
        self.fc2 = nn.Linear(64, 64)
        self.fc3 = nn.Linear(64, 1)

    def forward(self, state, action):
        x = torch.relu(self.fc1(torch.cat([state, action], 1)))
        x = torch.relu(self.fc2(x))
        q_value = self.fc3(x)
        return q_value

# Define DDPG agent
class DDPGAgent:
    def __init__(self, state_dim, action_dim, gamma=0.99, tau=0.001, lr_actor=0.001, lr_critic=0.001):
        self.actor = Actor(state_dim, action_dim)
        self.target_actor = Actor(state_dim, action_dim)
        self.critic = Critic(state_dim, action_dim)
        self.target_critic = Critic(state_dim, action_dim)

        # Initialize target networks with the same weights as the main networks
        self.target_actor.load_state_dict(self.actor.state_dict())
        self.target_critic.load_state_dict(self.critic.state_dict())

        # Define optimizers for actor and critic networks
        self.actor_optimizer = optim.Adam(self.actor.parameters(), lr=lr_actor)
        self.critic_optimizer = optim.Adam(self.critic.parameters(), lr=lr_critic)

        self.gamma = gamma
        self.tau = tau

    def select_action(self, state):
        state = torch.FloatTensor(state).unsqueeze(0)
        with torch.no_grad():
            action = self.actor(state)
        return action.cpu().numpy().flatten()
```

```python
def update(self, batch):
    states, actions, rewards, next_states, dones = batch

    # Compute Q target using target critic network
    next_actions = self.target_actor(next_states)
    target_q_values = self.target_critic(next_states, next_actions)
    q_targets = rewards + self.gamma * target_q_values * (1 - dones)

    # Update critic network
    q_values = self.critic(states, actions)
    critic_loss = nn.MSELoss()(q_values, q_targets.detach())
    self.critic_optimizer.zero_grad()
    critic_loss.backward()
    self.critic_optimizer.step()

    # Update actor network
    policy_actions = self.actor(states)
    actor_loss = -self.critic(states, policy_actions).mean()
    self.actor_optimizer.zero_grad()
    actor_loss.backward()
    self.actor_optimizer.step()

    # Update target networks with soft updates
    for target_param, param in zip(self.target_actor.parameters(), self.actor.parameters()):
        target_param.data.copy_(self.tau * param.data + (1 - self.tau) * target_param.data)

    for target_param, param in zip(self.target_critic.parameters(), self.critic.parameters()):
        target_param.data.copy_(self.tau * param.data + (1 - self.tau) * target_param.data)

# Main function for training the DDPG agent
def main():
    env = gym.make('Pendulum-v0')
    state_dim = env.observation_space.shape[0]
    action_dim = env.action_space.shape[0]
    agent = DDPGAgent(state_dim, action_dim)

    num_episodes = 1000
    batch_size = 64

    for episode in range(num_episodes):
        state = env.reset()
        total_reward = 0
        done = False

        while not done:
            action = agent.select_action(state)
            next_state, reward, done, _ = env.step(action)
            total_reward += reward

            # Store the transition in the replay buffer
            agent.update((state, action, reward, next_state, done))

            state = next_state

        print(f"Episode: {episode}, Total Reward: {total_reward}")

    env.close()

if __name__ == "__main__":
    main()
```

In this example, we implement a simple DDPG agent with actor and critic neural networks. The agent uses the actor network to select continuous actions for the given state. It interacts with the environment, stores the transitions in a replay buffer, and updates the actor and critic networks using the DDPG update rules.

Please note that this is a basic example to demonstrate the core concepts of DDPG in continuous action spaces. In practice, DDPG is often used with more complex neural network architectures, experience replay buffers, and other techniques to enhance performance and stability in more challenging environments.

Multi-agent reinforcement learning and hierarchical RL

Multi-agent reinforcement learning (MARL) is a subfield of reinforcement learning that deals with environments where multiple agents interact and learn simultaneously. In a MARL setting, each agent aims to maximize its own cumulative reward, which may or may not align with the goals of other agents. These agents may have access to different observations, actions, or reward signals, making the learning process more complex compared to single-agent RL.

Key Concepts of MARL:

1. **Centralized vs. Decentralized Policies:** In a multi-agent environment, agents can have centralized or decentralized policies. In centralized policies, agents have access to the observations and actions of other agents, enabling more coordination. In decentralized policies, each agent acts independently with limited information about the other agents.

2. **Cooperative vs. Competitive Scenarios:** MARL can involve cooperative settings where agents must work together to achieve common goals. Alternatively, it can involve competitive scenarios, where agents compete with each other, and their rewards may be in conflict.

3. **Communication and Coordination:** Some MARL algorithms allow agents to communicate or share information to improve coordination and collaboration. Communication can happen explicitly or implicitly through learned representations.

4. **Joint-Action Value Functions:** In MARL, the value function or Q-function becomes multi-agent, representing the joint value of all agents' actions. The Q-function needs to consider the interactions among agents to capture the environment's dynamics accurately.

5. **Learning Complexity:** MARL introduces challenges like non-stationarity (the environment changes as agents learn), credit assignment (assigning credit to agents for collective outcomes), and the curse of dimensionality (the state space grows exponentially with the number of agents).

6. **Emergent Behaviors:** In MARL, agents can exhibit emergent behaviors, where the interaction of multiple learning agents results in behaviors that were not explicitly programmed.

Hierarchical Reinforcement Learning (HRL):

Hierarchical Reinforcement Learning (HRL) is an RL approach that aims to deal with complex tasks by breaking them down into subtasks or hierarchies. HRL organizes agents into a hierarchy of policies, with high-level policies (also called options or macro-actions) controlling the agent's behavior over long time scales, and low-level policies handling shorter time-scale actions.

Key Concepts of HRL:

1. **Options:** In HRL, options are high-level policies that represent sequences of actions. Instead of directly selecting low-level actions, an agent can activate an option, which then executes a predefined sequence of actions until its termination.

2. **Intra-Option Policies:** Each option has its own set of intra-option policies, representing actions that the agent can take while executing the option. These intra-option policies are typically simpler compared to the original high-dimensional action space.

3. **Intra-Option Critic and Termination Conditions:** HRL includes an intra-option critic to estimate the value of an option and termination conditions to determine when an option should terminate and a new one should be selected.

4. **Learning Hierarchies:** In HRL, both high-level and low-level policies are learned simultaneously. High-level policies are

learned based on the success of completing subtasks, while low-level policies learn to execute actions efficiently given the high-level policies' instructions.

5. **Speeding up Learning:** HRL can significantly speed up learning by providing a structured way to explore the action space and focus on specific subtasks before learning the entire task.

Applications:

Both MARL and HRL have various real-world applications:

- MARL finds applications in collaborative multi-robot systems, traffic management, multi-player games, and resource allocation problems.

- HRL is useful in complex tasks like robot manipulation, autonomous driving, and game playing, where breaking tasks into subtasks can speed up learning and improve performance.

Overall, both MARL and HRL are essential areas of research in reinforcement learning that address challenges related to multiple interacting agents and complex tasks, respectively. They provide powerful tools for handling increasingly complex real-world scenarios.

EXAMPLE:

Let's provide an example that combines Multi-Agent Reinforcement Learning (MARL) and Hierarchical Reinforcement Learning (HRL). We'll consider a simple cooperative multi-agent task where two agents need to navigate through a maze to reach their respective goals while avoiding obstacles. The agents can use hierarchical policies to learn high-level strategies for navigating through the maze and low-level policies for taking individual actions.

Example: Cooperative Multi-Agent Maze Navigation using HRL

```python
import gym
import numpy as np
import torch
import torch.nn as nn
import torch.optim as optim

# Define the maze environment
class MazeEnvironment(gym.Env):
    def __init__(self, maze_size, num_agents):
        self.maze_size = maze_size
        self.num_agents = num_agents
        self.agent_positions = [(0, 0) for _ in range(num_agents)]
        self.goal_positions = [(maze_size - 1, maze_size - 1) for _ in range(num_agents)]

    def reset(self):
        self.agent_positions = [(0, 0) for _ in range(self.num_agents)]
        return self.agent_positions

    def step(self, actions):
        rewards = [0 for _ in range(self.num_agents)]
        dones = [False for _ in range(self.num_agents)]

        for i in range(self.num_agents):
            next_x, next_y = self.agent_positions[i]
            if actions[i] == 0:    # Move up
                next_x = max(0, next_x - 1)
            elif actions[i] == 1:    # Move down
                next_x = min(self.maze_size - 1, next_x + 1)
            elif actions[i] == 2:    # Move left
                next_y = max(0, next_y - 1)
            elif actions[i] == 3:    # Move right
                next_y = min(self.maze_size - 1, next_y + 1)

            if (next_x, next_y) not in self.agent_positions:
                self.agent_positions[i] = (next_x, next_y)

            if self.agent_positions[i] == self.goal_positions[i]:
                rewards[i] = 10
                dones[i] = True

        return self.agent_positions, rewards, dones, {}

# Define hierarchical actor and critic networks
class HierarchicalActor(nn.Module):
    def __init__(self, state_dim, option_dim):
        super(HierarchicalActor, self).__init__()
        self.fc1 = nn.Linear(state_dim, 64)
        self.fc2 = nn.Linear(64, option_dim)
```

```python
    def forward(self, state):
        x = torch.relu(self.fc1(state))
        option_value = self.fc2(x)
        return option_value

# Define the HRL agent
class HRLAgent:
    def __init__(self, state_dim, option_dim, num_options):
        self.hierarchical_actor = HierarchicalActor(state_dim, option_dim)
        self.hierarchical_critic = HierarchicalCritic(state_dim, option_dim)
        self.options = [i for i in range(num_options)]

        self.hierarchical_actor_optimizer = optim.Adam(self.hierarchical_actor.parameters(), lr=0.001)
        self.hierarchical_critic_optimizer = optim.Adam(self.hierarchical_critic.parameters(), lr=0.001)

    def select_option(self, state):
        state = torch.FloatTensor(state)
        with torch.no_grad():
            option_probs = self.hierarchical_actor(state)
            option = np.random.choice(self.options, p=option_probs.numpy())
        return option

    def update_hierarchical_networks(self, state, option_value):
        option_probs = self.hierarchical_actor(state)
        log_prob = torch.log(option_probs)
        loss = -log_prob * option_value
        self.hierarchical_actor_optimizer.zero_grad()
        self.hierarchical_critic_optimizer.zero_grad()
        loss.backward()
        self.hierarchical_actor_optimizer.step()
        self.hierarchical_critic_optimizer.step()

# Main function for training the HRL agent
def main():
    maze_size = 5
    num_agents = 2
    num_options = 4
    state_dim = 2 * num_agents
    option_dim = num_options

    env = MazeEnvironment(maze_size, num_agents)
    agent = HRLAgent(state_dim, option_dim, num_options)

    num_episodes = 1000
    max_steps = 100

    for episode in range(num_episodes):
        state = env.reset()
        total_reward = 0
        done = False

        for step in range(max_steps):
            options = [agent.select_option(state[i]) for i in range(num_agents)]

            # Execute options and get rewards and next states
            actions = [np.random.randint(4) for _ in range(num_agents)]  # Low-level actions (random for simplicity)
            next_state, rewards, dones, _ = env.step(actions)
```

```python
            # Update hierarchical networks using cumulative option value
            option_value = sum(rewards)
            agent.update_hierarchical_networks(state[0], option_value)

            state = next_state
            total_reward += sum(rewards)

            if all(dones):
                break

        print(f"Episode: {episode}, Total Reward: {total_reward}")

if __name__ == "__main__":
    main()
```

In this example, we have defined a simple cooperative multi-agent maze navigation environment where two agents aim to reach their respective goals. The agents use hierarchical actor-critic networks to learn high-level strategies (options) for navigating through the maze and low-level policies for taking individual actions. The agent learns by interacting with the environment and updating its hierarchical networks based on the cumulative value of the executed options.

Please note that this is a simplified example to demonstrate the concept of hierarchical reinforcement learning in a multi-agent setting. In practice, more complex environments and network architectures are used for better performance in real-world scenarios.

Chapter 8: Applications of Reinforcement Learning

Autonomous agents in robotics and self-driving cars

Autonomous agents in robotics and self-driving cars refer to intelligent systems that can make decisions and perform actions without direct human intervention. These agents are designed to operate autonomously in real-world environments, sensing their surroundings, processing information, and making decisions to achieve specific goals or tasks. The ultimate objective of autonomous agents is to perform tasks efficiently, safely, and adaptively without the need for constant human guidance.

Key Concepts of Autonomous Agents in Robotics and Self-Driving Cars:

1. **Perception and Sensing:** Autonomous agents rely on sensors such as cameras, LIDAR, radar, and other sensors to perceive and gather information about their environment. The collected sensory data is processed to understand the agent's surroundings and make informed decisions.

2. **Decision-Making and Planning:** The core capability of autonomous agents is their ability to make decisions and plan actions based on the perceived environment. They use algorithms, machine learning, and AI techniques to optimize their actions and navigate through complex scenarios.

3. **Control and Actuation:** Once the agent makes a decision, it needs to control its physical actions to execute the planned trajectory or behavior. In robotics, this involves controlling motors and actuators to move or manipulate the robot. In self-driving cars, it involves controlling the steering, acceleration, and braking.

4. **Safety and Risk Management:** Autonomous agents must prioritize safety and manage risks during their operation. They should be able to handle unexpected situations, avoid collisions,

and respond appropriately to dynamic changes in the environment.

5. **Localization and Mapping:** For effective navigation, autonomous agents often require knowledge of their own position (localization) and a map of the environment (mapping). They use techniques like Simultaneous Localization and Mapping (SLAM) to build and update their map while estimating their position within it.

6. **Machine Learning and Adaptation:** Autonomous agents often employ machine learning techniques to learn from data and improve their performance over time. Reinforcement Learning, Deep Learning, and other AI approaches are used to adapt the agent's behavior based on experience.

7. **Integration of High-Level Goals:** Autonomous agents typically operate with high-level goals or mission objectives. In self-driving cars, these goals may be defined by a destination or a series of waypoints. In robotics, the agent's objectives could include reaching a target location, completing a task, or interacting with humans in a collaborative manner.

Examples of Autonomous Agents:

1. **Self-Driving Cars:** Autonomous vehicles are perhaps the most well-known example of autonomous agents in action. Self-driving cars use various sensors, GPS, maps, and AI algorithms to navigate roads, avoid obstacles, and reach destinations safely.

2. **Autonomous Drones:** Drones equipped with sensors and computer vision capabilities can autonomously navigate and perform tasks like aerial surveillance, package delivery, or mapping large areas.

3. **Autonomous Robots in Manufacturing:** Robots used in manufacturing settings can be autonomous agents that perform tasks such as assembly, material handling, and quality inspection without direct human involvement.

4. **Autonomous Underwater and Aerial Vehicles:** These agents operate in challenging environments, such as underwater exploration or aerial monitoring, where human intervention is difficult or dangerous.

5. **Autonomous Unmanned Aerial Vehicles (UAVs):** UAVs used for various applications, including agriculture, search and rescue, and monitoring, are examples of autonomous agents that fly and execute tasks independently.

The development of autonomous agents in robotics and self-driving cars is an active and rapidly evolving field, driven by advances in artificial intelligence, machine learning, and robotics technologies. As these technologies progress, we can expect to see increasingly sophisticated and capable autonomous agents in various domains, contributing to improved efficiency, safety, and convenience in real-world applications.

Example: Self-Driving Car as an Autonomous Agent

Overview: A self-driving car is an advanced autonomous agent that uses a combination of sensors, computer vision, machine learning, and decision-making algorithms to navigate roads and complete various driving tasks without human intervention.

Components:

1. **Sensors:** A self-driving car is equipped with various sensors, including cameras, LIDAR (Light Detection and Ranging), radar, and ultrasonic sensors. These sensors provide a continuous stream of data about the car's surroundings, such as the positions of other vehicles, pedestrians, traffic signs, and road markings.

2. **Perception and Processing:** The self-driving car's onboard computer processes the sensor data using computer vision and other perception algorithms. This processing allows the car to

understand its environment and identify relevant objects and obstacles.

3. **Localization and Mapping:** Simultaneous Localization and Mapping (SLAM) techniques are used to create a map of the car's surroundings and simultaneously estimate the car's position within the map. This localization and mapping process help the car understand its position and plan its path accordingly.

4. **Decision-Making and Planning:** The self-driving car employs advanced decision-making algorithms, often based on machine learning and reinforcement learning, to plan its actions and navigate through complex traffic scenarios. It decides when to change lanes, turn at intersections, stop for pedestrians, and adjust its speed to follow traffic rules.

5. **Control and Actuation:** The car's control system translates the planned actions into physical movements, controlling the steering, acceleration, and braking. The control system ensures that the car follows the desired trajectory while maintaining stability and safety.

6. **Safety Features:** Self-driving cars are equipped with safety features such as collision detection and avoidance systems. These systems use the car's sensors and algorithms to detect potential collisions with other vehicles or obstacles and take evasive actions to avoid accidents.

Example Scenario: Let's consider a scenario where a self-driving car is navigating through a busy urban area.

1. **Sensing and Perception:** The car's sensors continuously scan the environment, detecting other vehicles, pedestrians, traffic signals, and lane markings.

2. **Localization and Mapping:** The car uses SLAM techniques to build a map of the surrounding area and determine its precise location within the map.

3. **Decision-Making and Planning:** Based on the sensor data and the map, the car's decision-making algorithm plans its path, taking into account traffic conditions, road rules, and safety considerations.

4. **Control and Actuation:** The control system translates the planned path into steering, acceleration, and braking commands. The car smoothly follows the planned trajectory while maintaining safe distances from other vehicles.

5. **Safety Features:** If the car detects a pedestrian crossing the road unexpectedly, the collision avoidance system may apply emergency braking to prevent an accident.

Advantages of Autonomous Agents in Self-Driving Cars:

1. **Safety:** Self-driving cars are designed to reduce human errors, which are a leading cause of accidents. Autonomous agents can respond faster and more consistently to potential hazards.

2. **Efficiency:** Self-driving cars can optimize driving patterns to reduce fuel consumption and minimize traffic congestion, leading to more efficient transportation.

3. **Accessibility:** Autonomous agents make driving accessible to people who are unable to drive due to age, disability, or other reasons.

4. **Productivity:** Self-driving cars free up passengers' time during travel, allowing them to be more productive or relax during their journey.

5. **Reduced Traffic Congestion:** With coordinated autonomous agents on the road, traffic flow can be optimized, leading to reduced congestion.

The development and deployment of self-driving cars as autonomous agents have the potential to revolutionize transportation and significantly improve road safety and efficiency. However, it also presents technical, ethical, and regulatory challenges that need to be carefully addressed for widespread adoption.

Game playing and strategic decision-making

Game playing and strategic decision-making are closely related concepts that involve making choices and forming strategies in competitive environments, particularly in the context of games and other multi-agent scenarios. These concepts are essential in various fields, ranging from recreational games to military planning and business strategy.

Game Playing:

In the context of artificial intelligence (AI), game playing refers to the use of AI techniques and algorithms to play games against human opponents or other AI agents. This includes classic board games like Chess and Go, video games, card games, and more. The objective of game playing AI is to make intelligent decisions and select moves that lead to favorable outcomes, such as winning the game or achieving specific game objectives.

Key Concepts of Game Playing AI:

1. **Search Algorithms:** Game playing AI often employs search algorithms, such as Minimax or Alpha-Beta Pruning, to explore possible future states and evaluate the best move to make based on a given evaluation function.

2. **Evaluation Functions:** An evaluation function is a key component of game playing AI that assesses the desirability of a game state. It assigns a numerical value to a position, indicating how favorable it is for the AI player. The AI aims to maximize its evaluation function while minimizing the opponent's.

3. **Depth of Search:** The depth to which the AI agent explores the game tree determines the sophistication of its strategic

decision-making. A deeper search explores more moves ahead but may require more computational resources.

4. **Heuristics:** In cases where complete search is not feasible, heuristics or rule-based strategies may be used to guide the AI's decision-making process.

Strategic Decision-Making:

Strategic decision-making involves analyzing a complex situation, anticipating the actions of others, and formulating a plan to achieve specific goals or objectives. It is not limited to game playing and can be applied in various contexts, such as business, military, politics, and sports.

Key Concepts of Strategic Decision-Making:

1. **Information Gathering:** In strategic decision-making, acquiring relevant information about the environment, competitors, or opponents is crucial for informed choices.

2. **Risk Assessment:** Strategic decisions often involve considering potential risks and uncertainties. Decision-makers evaluate the likelihood of different outcomes and their consequences.

3. **Long-term Planning:** Strategic decisions are usually made with a long-term perspective, considering the implications of choices over extended periods.

4. **Resource Allocation:** Decision-makers must allocate resources effectively to achieve their objectives while considering constraints.

Connection Between Game Playing and Strategic Decision-Making:

Game playing is a specific application of strategic decision-making, where the decisions are made within the context of games. Many concepts and techniques used in game playing AI, such as search algorithms and evaluation functions, are rooted in strategic decision-making principles.

Examples:

- In Chess and Go, AI agents use strategic decision-making to explore potential moves and select the most promising ones based on evaluations of board positions.

- In business strategy, companies use strategic decision-making to analyze markets, anticipate competitors' actions, and formulate plans for growth and competitive advantage.

- In military planning, strategic decision-making involves assessing the enemy's strengths and weaknesses, predicting their moves, and devising winning strategies.

- In sports, coaches and players engage in strategic decision-making to outwit opponents, adapt to changing game situations, and achieve victory.

Overall, game playing and strategic decision-making are fundamental aspects of human intelligence and have become important areas of study and application in the context of artificial intelligence and decision science. They provide valuable insights into how intelligent agents can make effective choices in competitive and dynamic environments.

Personalized recommendation systems and healthcare applications

What are Personalized Recommendation Systems? Personalized recommendation systems are AI-driven systems that provide tailored suggestions and recommendations to users based on their preferences, behavior, and historical interactions. These systems aim to deliver personalized content, products, or services to users, enhancing their experience and increasing engagement.

Key Concepts of Personalized Recommendation Systems:

1. **User Profiling:** Personalized recommendation systems create individual user profiles by analyzing user behavior, preferences, and historical data. They collect information about items users have interacted with, liked, or purchased.

2. **Collaborative Filtering:** One of the popular techniques used in recommendation systems is collaborative filtering, which identifies patterns of similarities between users and recommends items that similar users have enjoyed.

3. **Content-Based Filtering:** Another approach is content-based filtering, where recommendations are made based on the attributes of items and users' past preferences for similar attributes.

4. **Hybrid Approaches:** Many recommendation systems use hybrid approaches that combine collaborative filtering, content-based filtering, and other algorithms to provide more accurate and diverse recommendations.

5. **Reinforcement Learning:** In some cases, reinforcement learning is employed to optimize the recommendations by learning from user feedback and interactions.

6. **Real-Time Adaptation:** Personalized recommendation systems continuously update user profiles and adapt to changing preferences and behaviors in real-time.

Applications of Personalized Recommendation Systems:

1. **E-Commerce:** Personalized recommendation systems are commonly used in online shopping platforms to suggest products based on users' browsing and purchase history.

2. **Content Streaming Services:** Platforms like Netflix and Spotify use recommendation systems to suggest movies, TV shows, and songs that match users' tastes.

3. **Social Media:** Social media platforms use recommendation algorithms to display content, posts, and profiles that align with users' interests.

4. **News and Article Recommendations:** Media websites utilize recommendation systems to suggest news articles and content relevant to users' reading preferences.

5. **Travel and Hospitality:** In the travel industry, recommendation systems suggest personalized travel destinations, hotels, and activities based on user preferences.

Personalized Recommendation Systems in Healthcare Applications:

Healthcare Applications: In the context of healthcare, personalized recommendation systems can play a vital role in delivering tailored medical advice, treatment options, and health-related information to patients and healthcare providers.

Key Applications:

1. **Personalized Treatment Recommendations:** In healthcare, recommendation systems can analyze patient data, medical history, and genetic information to suggest personalized treatment plans and medications that are most effective for an individual's condition.

2. **Health and Wellness Recommendations:** Personalized recommendation systems can provide users with health and wellness suggestions based on their lifestyle, fitness goals, and medical needs.

3. **Medication and Adherence Management:** These systems can remind patients to take their medications, track adherence, and recommend adjustments to medication schedules.

4. **Clinical Decision Support:** Healthcare professionals can benefit from personalized recommendation systems that offer insights and suggestions to aid in diagnosis and treatment decisions.

5. **Disease Prevention and Early Detection:** Recommendation systems can analyze individual health data to identify potential health risks and recommend preventive measures and early screening tests.

6. **Precision Medicine:** Personalized recommendation systems are a crucial component of precision medicine, where treatments are tailored to an individual's unique genetic makeup and characteristics.

Benefits of Personalized Recommendation Systems in Healthcare:

1. **Improved Patient Outcomes:** Personalized recommendations can lead to more effective treatments and interventions, potentially improving patient outcomes and reducing healthcare costs.

2. **Enhanced Patient Engagement:** Personalized recommendations empower patients to take a proactive role in their healthcare decisions and promote active engagement in their health management.

3. **Efficient Healthcare Delivery:** By providing personalized insights and treatment options, recommendation systems can optimize healthcare delivery and resource allocation.

4. **Data-Driven Decision-Making:** These systems leverage vast amounts of patient data and medical knowledge to support evidence-based decision-making by healthcare providers.

5. **Continuous Learning:** Personalized recommendation systems can continuously learn from patient data, medical research, and treatment outcomes, enabling ongoing improvement in the recommendations provided.

As with any AI system used in healthcare, the development and deployment of personalized recommendation systems require careful attention to privacy, security, and ethical considerations to ensure patient confidentiality and data protection. When implemented responsibly, these systems have the potential to revolutionize healthcare by delivering personalized, precise, and effective medical recommendations and treatments.

Chapter 9: Ethical Considerations and Challenges

The impact of RL on society and ethical concerns

Reinforcement Learning (RL) is a powerful branch of artificial intelligence that has the potential to bring significant positive impacts on society, but it also raises important ethical concerns that need careful consideration. Understanding both the potential benefits and risks is essential for responsible and ethical implementation of RL technologies.

Impact of RL on Society:

1. **Automation and Efficiency:** RL can automate complex decision-making processes in various domains, leading to increased efficiency and productivity. For example, RL can optimize supply chain management, transportation logistics, and resource allocation, leading to cost savings and improved operations.

2. **Personalized Services:** RL can enable personalized services and recommendations, enhancing user experiences in areas like entertainment, e-commerce, and healthcare. By tailoring services to individual preferences, RL can provide more relevant and satisfying experiences for users.

3. **Healthcare Advancements:** RL has the potential to revolutionize healthcare by supporting personalized treatment plans, drug discovery, disease diagnosis, and medical image analysis. It can contribute to improved patient outcomes and more efficient healthcare delivery.

4. **Autonomous Systems:** RL is a fundamental technology behind the development of autonomous vehicles, drones, and robotic systems. These autonomous agents have the potential to enhance transportation, agriculture, exploration, and disaster response, making our world safer and more accessible.

5. **Scientific Discovery:** RL can be used to optimize experiments, conduct simulations, and accelerate scientific research. It

enables the discovery of new materials, drugs, and solutions to complex scientific problems.

Ethical Concerns and Challenges:

1. **Bias and Fairness:** RL algorithms are sensitive to biases in training data, leading to potential discrimination and unfair outcomes. If not carefully designed and audited, RL systems may perpetuate societal biases and inequalities.

2. **Safety and Risk Management:** The deployment of RL in safety-critical domains, such as autonomous vehicles and healthcare, raises concerns about system reliability, safety, and potential risks to human life.

3. **Transparency and Explainability:** RL models can be complex and difficult to interpret, making it challenging to understand their decision-making process. Lack of transparency raises concerns about accountability and trust in AI systems.

4. **Job Displacement:** As RL and automation technologies advance, there is concern over job displacement and the potential impact on the workforce. It may lead to unemployment and require re-skilling and job transitions for affected workers.

5. **Data Privacy and Security:** RL often relies on vast amounts of personal data, raising concerns about privacy breaches and data security. Ensuring proper data protection and user consent is critical to maintaining trust in RL systems.

6. **Ethical Decision-Making:** RL systems may encounter novel situations where the ethical course of action is unclear. Ensuring that RL models adhere to ethical guidelines and values is a challenge that requires careful consideration.

Ethical Considerations and Responsible AI:

1. **Bias Mitigation:** Developers must take measures to identify and address biases in training data, ensuring that RL models are fair and equitable.

2. **Safety and Security:** Safety should be a paramount concern when deploying RL in critical applications. Rigorous testing, validation, and fail-safe mechanisms are essential to minimize risks.

3. **Explainability and Transparency:** Efforts should be made to develop explainable RL models, allowing users to understand how decisions are made. Transparent AI systems can enhance user trust and enable accountability.

4. **Data Privacy:** Data collection and usage should comply with privacy regulations, and user consent must be obtained for data sharing and processing.

5. **Ethics by Design:** Ethical considerations should be embedded into the design and development of RL systems from the outset, emphasizing responsible and ethical AI practices.

6. **Public Engagement:** The development and deployment of RL technologies should involve public dialogue and engagement to ensure that societal values and concerns are taken into account.

By approaching RL with a commitment to ethical principles and responsible AI practices, we can harness its potential for positive societal impact while mitigating potential risks and challenges. Striking a balance between innovation and ethical responsibility is key to shaping a future where RL technologies contribute to the well-being of individuals and society as a whole.

Ensuring safety and avoiding harmful consequences

Ensuring safety and avoiding harmful consequences are crucial considerations when developing and deploying artificial intelligence (AI) systems, including those based on Reinforcement Learning (RL). As RL agents learn and interact with their environment, there is a risk of unintended negative outcomes or harmful behaviors. It is essential to implement safety measures and robust mechanisms to mitigate potential risks and ensure that RL systems operate responsibly.

Challenges in Ensuring Safety with RL:

1. **Sample Efficiency:** RL agents learn from interactions with the environment, and this learning process can be data-intensive and time-consuming. In safety-critical applications, it is crucial to ensure that agents can learn safely with minimal exposure to harmful situations.

2. **Safe Exploration:** During learning, RL agents explore the environment to discover optimal strategies. Safe exploration is necessary to avoid risky or unsafe actions that could lead to damage or adverse consequences.

3. **Adversarial Examples:** In some cases, malicious agents may intentionally manipulate RL systems by feeding them deceptive inputs, leading to harmful actions or vulnerabilities.

Safety Measures and Strategies for RL:

1. **Simulated Environments:** Simulated environments can be used to train RL agents in safe and controlled settings. This allows for extensive testing and experimentation without risks to the real world.

2. **Reward Shaping:** Designing appropriate reward functions is crucial in RL. By shaping the reward signals, developers can encourage desirable behaviors and discourage harmful actions.

3. **Constraint-based Learning:** Agents can be trained with constraints that explicitly forbid unsafe actions. This ensures that the agent adheres to safety rules during learning.

4. **Adversarial Testing:** RL systems can be subjected to adversarial testing, where potential vulnerabilities and harmful scenarios are simulated to assess the system's robustness.

5. **Model-Based Safety Checks:** Implementing safety checks at various stages of the RL pipeline helps identify potential risks and ensures that the agent follows safe trajectories.

6. **Human Oversight:** In safety-critical applications, human experts can provide oversight and intervene when necessary to prevent harmful actions.

7. **Interpretability and Explainability:** RL systems should be designed to be interpretable and explainable. This enables users to understand the agent's decision-making process and identify potential safety issues.

Addressing the Alignment Problem:

The alignment problem refers to the challenge of ensuring that an RL agent's objectives align with human values and intentions. Ensuring alignment is critical to prevent RL agents from pursuing objectives that may lead to unintended harmful consequences.

1. **Inverse Reinforcement Learning (IRL):** IRL is a technique where an RL agent learns the reward function from demonstrations provided by humans. This allows the agent to understand human intentions and align its behavior accordingly.

2. **Cooperative Inverse Reinforcement Learning (CIRL):** CIRL extends IRL to scenarios where the agent and the human collaboratively optimize the agent's behavior to meet shared objectives.

Safety-Aware RL and Robust AI:

Safety-aware RL and robust AI focus on designing AI systems that are resilient to uncertainties, adversarial attacks, and uncertainties in the environment. These approaches aim to improve the safety and reliability of RL systems in various applications.

Conclusion:

To ensure safety and avoid harmful consequences with RL, a multifaceted approach is required, encompassing robust algorithm design, safety measures, adversarial testing, human oversight, and ethical considerations. By adopting responsible AI practices and addressing safety concerns, we can harness the potential of RL for societal benefit while minimizing risks and negative impacts.

Responsible AI and the role of human oversight

Responsible AI refers to the ethical and principled development, deployment, and use of artificial intelligence systems to ensure that they align with human values, respect fundamental rights, and have a positive impact on individuals and society. Human oversight plays a critical role in ensuring responsible AI by providing checks, balances, and decision-making authority to guide and control AI systems.

The Role of Human Oversight in Responsible AI:

1. **Ethical Guidance:** Human oversight ensures that AI systems are developed and deployed in alignment with ethical principles, legal frameworks, and societal norms. It helps AI developers consider the broader implications of their technology on various stakeholders.

2. **Bias Mitigation:** Humans can identify and correct biases in AI systems, ensuring fair and unbiased decision-making. They can review and modify training data to reduce discriminatory outcomes.

3. **Value Alignment:** Human oversight ensures that AI systems align with human values and intentions. It allows for customization of AI behavior based on the preferences and needs of individuals or organizations.

4. **Complex Decision-Making:** In complex and sensitive situations, human judgment is vital. AI systems may lack the ability to fully

comprehend nuanced ethical or moral dilemmas, and human oversight can fill this gap.

5. **Context Awareness:** Human overseers possess context awareness and common sense, which helps interpret ambiguous situations and avoid inappropriate responses by AI systems.

6. **Legal and Regulatory Compliance:** Human oversight ensures that AI applications comply with applicable laws, regulations, and industry standards. It helps avoid legal risks and ensures accountability.

7. **Transparency and Explainability:** Humans can demand transparency from AI systems and assess their decision-making process. Human oversight ensures that AI models are explainable, enabling users to understand how decisions are reached.

8. **Risk Mitigation:** Human oversight helps identify and mitigate potential risks and vulnerabilities in AI systems. It can involve continuous monitoring and evaluation to ensure the safety and reliability of AI deployments.

9. **Responsible Innovation:** Human oversight encourages responsible innovation in AI. It encourages researchers and developers to consider the societal implications of their work and find solutions to mitigate negative impacts.

10. **Contingency Planning:** Humans can develop contingency plans in case of AI system failures or unexpected behavior. Human overseers can intervene if the AI system exhibits undesirable actions.

Challenges of Human Oversight in AI:

1. **Scalability:** Human oversight may be challenging to scale, especially for large-scale AI systems or platforms with extensive user interactions.

2. **Expertise:** Human overseers must possess the necessary expertise in AI, ethics, and relevant domains to effectively evaluate and guide AI systems.

3. **Bias of Human Decision-Makers:** Human overseers themselves may introduce biases in the oversight process, impacting the AI system's fairness and objectivity.

4. **Automation and Autonomy:** In fully autonomous AI systems, the level of human oversight may be limited, which raises concerns about accountability and control.

5. **Privacy Concerns:** Human oversight requires access to data and AI decision-making processes, which may raise privacy and security concerns.

Conclusion:

Human oversight is a critical component of responsible AI, ensuring that AI systems are developed, deployed, and used in an ethical and socially responsible manner. While there are challenges in implementing human oversight, its role in guiding AI decisions, promoting transparency, mitigating risks, and aligning AI with human values makes it an indispensable element in building a trustworthy and beneficial AI ecosystem. Responsible AI with robust human oversight can foster public trust and confidence in AI technologies and foster their positive impact on society.

Conclusion

Encouraging readers to explore and contribute to the field of Reinforcement Learning

Encouraging readers to explore and contribute to the field of Reinforcement Learning (RL) is essential for fostering innovation and progress in this area of artificial intelligence. RL is a dynamic and exciting field that holds tremendous potential for solving complex real-world problems. By inspiring and empowering individuals to engage with RL, we can drive advancements, discover novel applications, and tackle significant challenges. Here are some ways to encourage readers to explore and contribute to the field of RL:

1. **Education and Learning Resources:** Providing accessible and comprehensive learning resources, such as online tutorials, courses, and books, can help readers understand the fundamentals of RL. These resources should cater to beginners as well as experienced researchers, making RL knowledge available to a broad audience.

2. **Hands-on Projects:** Encourage readers to undertake hands-on RL projects to gain practical experience. Open-source RL frameworks and libraries, such as TensorFlow and PyTorch, allow individuals to implement RL algorithms and experiment with various environments.

3. **Competitions and Challenges:** Organizing RL competitions and challenges can motivate readers to apply their skills and knowledge in solving specific problems. Competitions foster healthy competition and collaboration among participants.

4. **Research Communities and Conferences:** Readers can benefit from engaging with RL research communities and attending conferences like NeurIPS, ICML, and RL-specific events. These platforms offer opportunities to network, share ideas, and stay updated on the latest research trends.

5. **Mentorship and Collaboration:** Encourage experienced RL practitioners to offer mentorship and guidance to newcomers.

Collaborative projects can bridge knowledge gaps and provide a supportive environment for learning and growth.

6. **Communication and Outreach:** Encourage readers to share their experiences and knowledge with others. Contributing to blogs, forums, or open-source projects fosters a culture of knowledge sharing and community-building.

7. **Multidisciplinary Applications:** Highlight the interdisciplinary nature of RL and its applications in various domains like robotics, finance, healthcare, gaming, and more. Illustrate how RL can contribute to solving real-world challenges across diverse fields.

8. **Ethical Considerations:** Emphasize the importance of ethical considerations in RL research and applications. Encourage readers to think critically about the societal impact of RL systems and promote responsible AI practices.

9. **Public Awareness:** Promote public awareness of RL advancements and their potential benefits. Demonstrate how RL can positively impact people's lives and address global challenges.

10. **Continuous Learning and Adaptation:** Encourage readers to stay curious and continuously learn about the evolving trends and breakthroughs in RL. As RL is an active research area, staying updated is crucial for contributing meaningfully.

By promoting exploration, collaboration, and ethical considerations, we can create a vibrant and inclusive RL community that drives innovation and addresses pressing societal needs. Encouraging readers to engage with RL will not only expand their knowledge but also contribute to the collective effort in advancing AI and shaping a better future.

Final thoughts and words of encouragement for aspiring RL practitioners

To aspiring Reinforcement Learning (RL) practitioners, embarking on a journey in this exciting field of artificial intelligence opens up a world of possibilities and opportunities for innovation and impact. Here are some final thoughts and words of encouragement to inspire and support your pursuit of RL:

1. Embrace the Learning Journey: RL can be challenging, but don't be discouraged by initial complexities. Embrace the learning journey and start with the fundamentals. With dedication and persistence, you'll gradually grasp the concepts and gain the confidence to tackle more complex RL problems.

2. Hands-On Practice Matters: Theory is essential, but hands-on practice is equally crucial. Dive into RL projects, experiment with code, and gain practical experience. Implement RL algorithms, work with different environments, and learn from your successes and failures.

3. Emphasize Problem-Solving: Focus on understanding problems and their contexts. RL is a powerful tool for solving real-world challenges. Train your mind to think creatively about how RL techniques can be applied to various domains and make a positive impact.

4. Collaborate and Engage: Join RL research communities, forums, and conferences to connect with like-minded individuals. Collaborate with peers, seek mentorship from experienced practitioners, and engage in discussions that broaden your perspective.

5. Stay Curious and Updated: RL is a rapidly evolving field. Stay curious and keep up with the latest research and advancements. Be open to exploring emerging trends and novel approaches in RL.

6. Explore Interdisciplinary Applications: RL is versatile and applicable across diverse fields. Look beyond traditional domains and explore interdisciplinary applications in areas like robotics, finance, healthcare, and sustainability.

7. Ethical Considerations are Vital: As you contribute to RL research and applications, keep ethical considerations at the forefront. Strive to build AI systems that are fair, transparent, and accountable, and be mindful of the societal impact of your work.

8. Celebrate Progress and Learn from Setbacks: Celebrate your progress, no matter how small. Acknowledge that setbacks and challenges are part of the learning process. Learn from them, adapt, and use them as stepping stones to grow.

9. Share Knowledge and Inspire Others: As you gain expertise in RL, share your knowledge with others. Contribute to the community through blogs, tutorials, or open-source projects. Inspire and mentor newcomers, fostering a culture of knowledge-sharing.

10. Have Confidence in Your Abilities: Believe in your abilities and have confidence in your potential to make a difference. Your unique perspective and ideas can contribute to the advancement of RL and the broader AI community.

Remember that the journey in RL is about continuous learning and growth. Be patient with yourself, and don't shy away from challenges. As you explore RL and contribute to the field, you are part of a collective effort that is shaping the future of AI and pushing the boundaries of what is possible. Embrace the adventure, and let your passion for RL drive you toward fulfilling experiences and impactful contributions. The world of RL eagerly awaits your creativity and innovative spirit!

www.ingramcontent.com/pod-product-compliance
Lightning Source LLC
Chambersburg PA
CBHW070116010626
45794CB00013B/1951